COP SPEAK

*The Lingo of
Law Enforcement
and Crime*

Tom Philbin

John Wiley & Sons, Inc.
New York . Chichester . Brisbane . Toronto . Singapore

Copyright © 1996 by Tom Philbin
Published by John Wiley & Sons, Inc.

ISBN 0-471-04304-4

Printed in the United States of America

10 9 8 7 6 5 4 3 2 1

Preface

This book is part dictionary, part encyclopedia, part etymological tract, and hopefully all entertaining. It rounds up law enforcement lingo, the language that police use in their everyday work.

The terms and phrases delve into all aspects of police work, from homicide to traffic tickets, and unearth the unique patois that police use. "Police" here refers not only to urban and suburban police but also to the "feds"—agents for the Federal Bureau of Investigation, Bureau of Alcohol, Tobacco and Firearms, Drug Enforcement Agency, Secret Service, Postal Authorities, and other groups such as prison officers.

Sometimes the terminology is raw (an autopsy is described as *making a canoe*); sometimes it is official-sounding (*perpetrator*); sometimes it is almost laughably euphemistic (such as describing a mass murderer as an *offender*).

But police use their lingo because it effectively communicates their thoughts and ideas clearly and quickly. For example, if you are a police officer in New York City and you call in a *ten thirteen,* all cops within hearing distance will drop what they're doing and rush to your aid. Brief, chilling, and very clear to those who hear and understand it, *ten thirteen* in New York City means "officer needs assistance."

While most of the lingo is generated by cops, a good portion comes from *bad guys.* The police have adopted criminal terminology because it is quick and effective, particularly when trying to communicate with bad guys. For example, an East Los Angeles police officer interrogating a gang member about whether another gang member uses cocaine won't ask, "Is he using cocaine?" The officer would more likely ask, "Is he a cluckhead?" because *cluckhead* is the term used in the 'hood (neighborhood) to describe a user of crack cocaine.

Law enforcement lingo comes in and out of vogue and can vary by location. For example, in the East any homicide that goes over forty-eight hours without being solved is called a *mystery;* in the Midwest it's called a *whodunit.* In both regions, police would agree that such cases are much harder to *clear* (solve) than *grounders* (easy cases to solve). Some terms are of recent vintage, and some go back halfway to forever. *Felon,* for example, started its etymological journey back in the Middle Ages when it described a person who was "full of venom." Police would still agree that holds true.

But much cop talk is universal. If you are a perpetrator in Broken Rifle, Colorado, you will be a perpetrator in Boston, Massachusetts, in San Diego, California, and in Nome, Alaska.

Cop lingo is not without humor; on the contrary, more than a little of it contains humor, some of it grisly, some of it nasty, some just plain funny. In Chicago a person who jumps off a building has done a *dry dive*. And what do cops in New York call arson? *Jewish lightning.* Mexicans might laugh at that, until they learn that California cops call arson *Mexican lightning.*

In doing this book, I picked the brains of many law enforcement people and scoured—or should I say *canvassed*—a lot of written matter. By far the most helpful, particularly when it comes to etymology, is the *Oxford English Dictionary*—twenty-one volumes that can fairly be described as a stupendous work. I used it a lot yet cumulatively extracted only part of a drop from a bucket.

I want to thank all the folks who helped me, as well as myself! Over the years I have written thirteen cop books, both fiction and nonfiction, and I come from a family of cops, from whom I have picked up more than a few terms. I hope that what I knew before I started has helped flavor and enrich what I've written.

Indeed, I hope people who read the book will delight in it as I truly did (when I wasn't gulping at the immensity of my task) when doing the research. I think I can safely say that if they happen to hear a dialogue between cops, such as the following, they will, after reading this book, be able to instantly translate it.

> *"Hey, Matt, you're catching now, right?"* (Your turn to take the next case, right?)
>
> *"Yeah, loo. But I was going to do some more KOD on the Perez thing. I think we can clear that soon."* (Yes, lieutenant. But I was going to do some more canvassing—knocking on doors—on the Perez case. I think we can solve it soon.)
>
> *"Forget it for now. Some maggot did a mule out by the airport.* (Some criminal murdered a drug courier.) *Take that. I got the residence address right here."*

Have fun.

Tom Philbin

How To Use This Book

This is a dictionary of the *lingo* of law enforcement and crime. If you look up a "straight" term, you will be cross-referenced to its most common slang equivalent. For instance, if you look up **marijuana,** you will be referred to **pot,** where you will find not only a definition of that slang term but also basic information on marijuana and a list of dozens of its slang equivalents.

Related words of interest are cross-referenced at the end of each entry. Relevant words within an entry that are defined elsewhere in this book are written in italic *CAPITAL LETTERS*.

Simple definitions are given for each term, and, as much as possible, enriching details that relate to it. For example, look under **mass murder,** and you'll find not only a definition but a brief discussion, including when and where the term came into existence or at least into the public consciousness: One beautiful day in September 1949 Howard Unruh, dressed in a neat suit and bow tie, walked down a Camden, New Jersey, street and shot thirteen people to death.

There is also etymology included for terms whose origins are not so obvious. For example, the deadly dumdum bullets were named for a town near Calcutta where they were produced around the turn of the century. Also, if a term includes a published citation and date, you can assume that is the first time the term was used in print. Some terms failed to give up their etymological roots despite vigorous digging by the author. Two such are **Mickey Finn** and **burglar,** but they are well in the minority.

Acknowledgments

I'm very grateful for the help I received in compiling the terms for this book. I am particularly grateful to Steve Malandrino, Jamie Mills, Jessy Flynn, Howard Kim, Jack Sturiano, Gary Messina Sr., Franky Garrido, Charlie Hudson, Tony Romano, Ed Grilli, Kathleen Scott, Ed Bambauer, John Dowd, and Monica Foderingham Brown of the NYPD Academy Library. I would also like to thank those great reference librarians at the Harborfields (N.Y.) Public Library, who have the same instincts as nurses when it comes to helping people—and the tenacity of pit bulls when it comes to getting an author what he needs.

Thanks also to PJ Dempsey, Senior Editor at John Wiley, who bought the book way back when. And last, and most of all, thanks to Chris Jackson, a brilliant young editor who worked long and hard with me (and by himself) to bring the book to where it is. Thank you, Chris.

A

Abe

Five dollars' worth of illegal drugs.

The term refers to the image of Abraham Lincoln found on a $5 bill.

accelerant

A flammable substance used in the commission of arson.

A variety of materials are used as accelerants, including grease, wax paper, kerosene, charcoal lighter fluid, paint thinner, grain alcohol, and of course gasoline. Arson investigators say that grain alcohol is becoming the accelerant of choice. Because it is also used to *FREEBASE* cocaine, it is well known and easily available.

acid

See *LSD*.

acid head

A habitual user of *LSD*.

acquaintance rape

A rape committed by someone known to the victim.

Rapes committed by men who know their victims are far more common than is generally believed: 50 percent of all rapes are carried out by men who know their victims either well or casually.

One myth is that such rapes are somehow less disturbing to the victim than those called *STRANGER RAPES*. In fact, women who are victims of acquaintance rape generally suffer a greater sense of betrayal and shock than those who are assaulted by a stranger.

Acquaintance rape, also known as "date rape" and "confidence rape," has come into more prominence in the last 10 or 15 years, since rape itself has been under more scrutiny.

ADA

Assistant district attorney.

ADAs are lawyers assigned to prosecute the myriad cases resulting from arrests by police officers. Many ADAs, after sufficient experience working on the prosecutorial side of the law, quit and become defense attorneys because the pay is better.

adiosis (state of)

In Suffolk County, New York, police description of someone who has just died or is about to.

"Adiosis" is derived from *adiós,* the Spanish term used to express farewell.

This jocular expression is usually used at the scene of a *FATAL* (motor vehicle accident involving death). One police officer might say to another, "How's he doing?" and be met with the response, "He's in a state of adiosis."

advise

To tell, notify, or inform.

Police never say or tell anything; they advise.

agonies

Drug withdrawal symptoms.

The origin of this term is not clear, but it certainly accurately describes what one can go through during drug withdrawal.

Withdrawal symptoms differ depending on the drug. For instance, while *LSD* has no known withdrawal symptoms, withdrawing from cocaine or heroin can cause watery eyes, runny nose, loss of appetite, insomnia, irritability, tremors, panic, cramps, nausea, chills, and sweating. Withdrawing from a depressant drug like Quaaludes *('LUDES)* can result in delirium, convulsions, even death.

See also *BABE, COLD TURKEY, CRASH,* and *KICK.*

airmail

Concrete, bricks, and the like hurled down from rooftops onto patrol cars responding to a call.

algor mortis

The cooling of the body after death.

How quickly a body cools depends on many factors, but it generally takes about forty hours for a corpse to cool to the air temperature outside the body. Over the first few hours body temperature drops 3 to 3.5 degrees per hour, then one degree per hour until it stabilizes at the temperature outside the body.

In fiction it always seems possible to determine exact time of death by scientific means, but this is rarely possible in the real world because of several variables, including temperature. For example, the body temperature will change much more rapidly in warm weather than in cold, because destructive bacteria grow faster in warm weather.

See also *RIGOR* and *STIFF.*

alligator effect

In arson, the alligator-skin appearance of burned wood that has been doused with a liquid *ACCELERANT.*

One way that arson investigators can tell if a fire is the work of a *TORCH* is to look for alligatoring. The fire burns deeper where gasoline or another accelerant has been poured, and the wood takes on the appearance described.

amped

Under the influence of the stimulant drug amphetamine.

The term is a shortened form of the words *amphetamine* and "amperage" (the strength of an electrical current passing through a wire, measured in amperes).

The effect of amphetamines is physiologically electric. Someone who is amped experiences excitation, euphoria, increased alertness and pulse rate, elevated blood pressure, insomnia, and loss of appetite.

Someone who has overdosed on amphetamines is said to have *overamped.*

See also *SPEED.*

amphetamine

See *SPEED.*

amyl nitrate

Common name for amyl nitrite.

See *POPPERS*.

angel

An influential person of importance who has a personal, familial, political, or other close binding relationship with a police officer.

This could be a high-ranking officer in a department, a powerful politician, or perhaps an influential community leader. No police department is without politics, and the person who has an angel is that much better off when it comes to promotions, transfers, or even sweeping some matter under the rug.

See also *RABBI* and *HOOK*.

APB

All points bulletin.

Sent from police headquarters to all its commands simultaneously, this message means that something urgent is happening, such as a suspect fleeing from the site of a *HEIST*.

Also called a *citywide* in certain regions, including New York City.

arrest

See *COLLAR, FALL, KEEPER,* and *PINCH*.

"Assume the position."

The standard command given by cops to suspects who are to be searched.

The position is leaning forward with hands against a wall and feet wide apart. It is designed to keep the suspect off balance, hamper quick movement, and facilitate safe searching. Police have to be particularly careful when searching a suspect, because while concentrating on the search they can lose sight of potential danger.

Even a suspect who seems relatively calm may be desperate, such as a murderer or drug dealer who is facing life in prison or execution. One major mistake is to let a suspect assume the position in front of a reflective surface, such as a window; doing so allows a suspect to see a police officer's actions and possibly seize an opportunity for disabling the officer.

The more secure positions to have suspects assume include kneeling down and doing a *PRONE OUT.*

A.T. and F.

The Bureau of Alcohol, Tobacco and Firearms; also known as the *B.A.T. and F.* ("bat and eff").

attitude adjustment

Illegal brute force used to make a suspect or *PERP* comply with the demands of the police.

According to one cop, "When a cop says 'He needs an attitude adjustment,' he means the bad guy needs the crap knocked out of him."

See also *TUNE 'EM UP.*

autoeroticism

Tying or otherwise constraining oneself for sexual stimulation.

People who engage in this tie themselves up, exquisitely and carefully, arranging gradual strangulation and loss of air supply while staying in full control. It is said that the absence of oxygen increases the extent and intensity of orgasm, which the participant achieves by masturbation. But sometimes the participant loses control, and that's when the *ME* (medical examiner) or coroner shows up.

Rope need not be used. For example, a factory guard wrapped himself in large plastic sheets, had a snorkel tube to breathe through, and had a knife to cut himself out in case something went wrong. Something did—he lost the snorkel tube—but he was unable to cut himself free before being asphyxiated.

It is almost always males who practice this form of auto-eroticism.

B

babe

Drug used for detoxification.

When an addict is trying to withdraw from drugs, doctors often administer other drugs to lessen the physiological impact on the body. The most common drug used to treat addicts is methadone, which is effective chiefly in heroin withdrawal.

In a planned treatment program, a drug like methadone is administered in a context of therapy and education and in conjunction with family or other support. Addicts, like alcoholics, are never considered cured.

The origin of babe is obscure, but the term does suggest warmth and support, just as a baby might receive from its mother.

See also *AGONIES, COLD TURKEY,* and *KICK.*

baby raper

Prison slang for child molester.

In prison there is a hierarchy of convicts based in part on the crime committed. Near the bottom of this pecking order is the child molester. Other prisoners loathe these inmates, perhaps because some prisoners have children themselves and can imagine their own children as being prey. More likely, some psychologists say, prison is such an ego-debilitating place that prisoners often shore up their own self-image by tearing down other prisoners. The only convict in the prison hierarchy lower than the child molester is the *SNITCH.* Being a child molester can be precarious for one's health in prison, but being a snitch can be a death sentence.

baby-sit

To guide someone through their first drug experience; usually done by an experienced user.

See also *GROUND CONTROL*.

back gate parole

Death of a prisoner.

backing

Protection or support provided an inmate by other prisoners.

Some convicts require protection in prison because they are not able to defend themselves against the predatory practices of others. Such "defenseless" convicts may be old, infirm to some degree, or, those at greatest risk, young and attractive but not physically or mentally tough.

Protection in prison comes at a price. For example, a white inmate can become a member of the Aryan Nation, a group of white prisoners who espouse the supremacy of the white race. But it is made clear that membership takes precedence over everything else, including family. In a sense the convict vows loyalty to the Nation much as a *MADE MAN* vows loyalty to the Mafia.

Backing may also be bought for sexual favors.

See also *JOCKER* and *MAYTAG*.

backup

A reinforcing unit or individual officer who will come to a police officer's aid if necessary.

A typical backup situation would be in a *BUY AND BUST* operation where an officer poses as a drug buyer and/or dealer. If things go well, backup is not needed; if things turn sour, backup can mean the difference between life and death.

Another backup situation would be when police partners approach a building in search of a suspect. One officer may enter the building while the other waits outside in case the suspect tries to exit unseen.

backstrap

Telephone hookup that bookmakers use to avoid apprehension.

This is also called a black box. One or more phones will be installed in an empty house, and then telephone wire will be run to additional phones at a location where the bookmaker is actually present. When bettors call in their bets, they are automatically connected to the second location. When the police raid the first location, they find it empty; by the time they get another search warrant and find the second location, the bookmaker will likely have fled.

badger game

1. In general, extortion.
2. A con game where a female entices a male into a sexually compromising situation, after which an accomplice will come forth to blackmail the victim.

The term derives from a cruel and sadistic sport of the 1800s called the badger game or "drawing," in which a badger would be enticed or driven out of its hole to suddenly face a fight to the death with dogs.

bad go

Bad reaction to a drug.

Drugs may have unintended short- and long-term side effects. Heroin creates feelings of euphoria but can also produce nausea, respiratory depression, and even death. Cocaine can be similarly lethal. Marijuana can cause memory loss and disorientation.

Drugs can also produce negative psychological effects, depending on a complex of factors. For example, cocaine is a stimulant that usually elevates mood, but in people who are already depressed it may induce deeper depression.

bad guys

Criminals.

bag

1. In New York City, the name for the winter uniform.

The NYPD winter uniform has not changed much in decades. It is dark blue, made of wool, heavy, and shapeless. As it gets older, it begins to bulge and look baggy, hence the name.

Officers get an allowance to take care of the uniforms, but as one patrolman put it, "You're not starting with something out of *GQ* to begin with."

2. A packet of drugs.

3. To arrest.

The term comes from the concept of being captured, much as a small animal is trapped by means of a bag.

See also *COLLAR*, *KEEPER*, and *FALL*.

bag bride

A prostitute who smokes crack cocaine.

The term most likely comes from the bags that drugs come in, as well as the disheveled and dilapidated look that prostitutes on drugs eventually assume.

Also known as *skeeger*, *skeezer*, and *coke whore*.

bag man

1. *DRUG DEALER*. The term is derived from the practice of selling drugs in bags.

2. Person who transports money generated by gambling or drugs.

See also *MULE*.

bag the hands

Encase the hands of a homicide victim in bags.

Bagging the hands of a homicide victim is standard procedure. This helps preserve any *TRACE MATERIAL*, such as skin or hair, that might be on the hands or under the fingernails of the victim. When a victim is fighting for his or her life, a natural reaction is to defend with the hands, scratching or grabbing the perpetrator. Minute quantities of the material that may be found on the victim's hands can be crucial in identifying the guilty person through *DNA* tests.

Movies or television often shows the victim's hands bagged in some sort of plastic wrap or plastic baggie, but real-life investigators prefer paper bags because plastic tends to speed up putrefaction, thus cutting into time for analysis. In addition, plastic does not allow the hands to "breathe," and the lack of air may alter the trace evidence significantly.

baller

A highly successful *DRUG DEALER* or *dope pusher.*

This term is used primarily in the Los Angeles area.
See also *BARNES MAN.*

B & D

Bondage and domination sexual activities.

In B & D one person plays a submissive role, the M (masochist), while the other is dominant, or S (sadist).

Police are interested in B & D because (1) it's a crime if prostitutes are involved and (2) it can sometimes provide leads in future police investigation. For example, if someone who practices B & D is murdered, police would immediately want to know who the victim's partner or partners were, particularly if the investigation revealed evidence of B & D at the crime scene.

B and E

See *BURGLARY.*

B and E man

See *BURGLAR.*

banker

Someone who receives and holds the cash received from drug sales.

barbs

Short for barbiturates, one of a family of drugs characterized as depressants.

Barbiturates are not popular on the street because they take a relatively long time to take effect—15 to 40 minutes. For the street user who wants a high "last Thursday," as one narcotics officer put it, this is an eternity.

Barbs produce various feelings depending on the specific kinds used. Synthesized from barbituric acid, there are some 2,500 derivatives but only about 15 in use. Some act as sedatives, and serious problems—including death—arise when barbiturates are combined with alcohol.

Barbs aren't ordinarily sold on the street, but they are available with a prescription.

One potent statement about what barbiturates can do is indicated by their use by veterinarians to euthanize animals.

bargain plea

See *PLEA BARGAIN*.

Barnes man

A major *DRUG DEALER*.

In Harlem in the 1970s and 1980s there was a major drug dealer named Nicky Barnes. He was eventually caught and convicted and, facing many years in prison, *FLIPPED* (testified against his colleagues) to shorten his own sentence.

See also *BALLER*.

barricaded EDP

See *HOSTAGE TAKER*.

basehead

See *FREEBASE*.

B.A.T. and F.

See *A.T. and F.*

baton

The club or stick that police officers carry.

The term for baton differs from locality to locality. In many places it is commonly called a *nightstick* or *billy club*.

Because they are occasionally used against people, all batons share one characteristic: They are made of extremely hard wood, such as locust or rosewood, whose strength ensures against cracking midway through a melee.

There was a time in the 1800s when police officers carried only batons for preserving the peace (this is still the case in England), but criminals in America eventually became rougher and police began wearing sidearms.

beat

The area a police officer is assigned to patrol, either in a radio car or on foot.

The term describes the repetitive nature of the job. It goes back to at least the early 1800s; in Thackeray's *Ball Policeman* (1879), an officer talks of how he "paced upon my beat with steady step and slow." Also known as *foot post*.

See also *PORTABLES*.

beat cops

Police who work a particular *BEAT*, as opposed to working in several areas.

For many years officers would walk the same beat for their entire careers; this gave them intimate knowledge of the beat and the citizens who lived there. Over the years police departments have tried various special squads that created a gap between the police and citizenry. Now, in general, it is fair to say that the pendulum has swung the other way and more cops are back on the beat.

See also *PORTABLES*.

bedbugs

Drug addicts.

beef

1. A problem a police officer has with a criminal or suspected criminal.

   The term has been used to describe a complaint in standard English since at least 1900. The *Oxford English Dictionary* carries a quote from *Fables in Slang* by Ade (1899): "He made a Horrible Beef because he couldn't get Loaf Sugar for his Coffee."

   See also *COMPLAINT* and *SQUEAL*.

2. A specific criminal charge.

   "What's the beef?" a suspect might ask a detective; "Murder One" might be the response.

being on eyeball

In female prisons, watching someone who is perceived as a suicide risk.

belt

The effect caused by a drug.

Most drugs are taken strictly for their mind-altering effects, such as mood change, excitement, relaxation, pleasure, analgesis, stimulation, or sedation.

bender

Drug party.

Classically, this term applied to a long alcoholic siege, but in recent years it has come to be applied to drug taking.

See also *BREAK NIGHT* and *RAVE.*

Bernie (a)

In the New York area, a potential crime victim who may look like easy prey to criminals but is emphatically not.

"Bernie" refers to Bernhard Goetz, a mild-looking bespectacled man who was approached on a New York City subway train on December 22, 1984, by four youths—three brandishing long sharpened screwdrivers—who asked for cigarettes and money. Goetz, who had been mugged twice before, reached into his pocket, and instead of coming out with money, produced a nine-millimeter automatic, which he used to shoot all four youths. He then beat a hasty retreat.

The climate at the time was such that according to some polls, over 50 percent approved of Goetz's vigilantism, even though one of the youths, Darrell Cabey, was paralyzed from the waist down. Some suggested that Goetz had overreacted, firing at the youths when they were defenseless (and he used the nasty *HOLLOW POINT BULLETS).*

Goetz subsequently gave himself up to Concord, New Hampshire, police. There followed a series of trials—amid much furor—that essentially resulted in Goetz receiving a slap on the wrist. One of the four youths sued Goetz for $50 million but lost the case.

big bitch

See *BITCH.*

big store

Any con game in which a store is required to bring the con off.

These days most stings are perpetrated not by criminals but by law enforcement agencies, who periodically set up shop in some illegal activity to net criminals. *IAD* (Internal Affairs Division) units in *PD*s also set up stings to catch *DIRTY* cops.

billy club

See *BATON.*

bindle

A small package of drugs.

A bindle is a common unit of a drug sale.

bing

Enough drugs for a single injection.

bit

A prison sentence.

"He's doing a bit in Sing Sing," the statement might go.

See also *DIME* and *NICKEL.*

bitch

A conviction based on being a habitual criminal.

In standard English, the word "bitch" means female dog, and over time it has developed very strong negative connotations. Hence it is used to describe a conviction based on habitual criminal behavior, which at the least means a very long prison sentence or perhaps life. It's also known as a *big bitch.*

bite marks

Marks made by human teeth in an assault.

Over the last twenty years or so, homicide investigation has gotten more sophisticated and has come to rely on expertise outside of what was once considered standard police investigative technique. One of these new experts is the forensic dentist or odontologist, a person who can craft a profile of a killer based on the type and severity of the bite marks on the victim. Teeth are unique from one person to the next. The testimony given by a forensic odontologist helped convict the infamous serial murderer Ted Bundy, who often bit the buttocks and other parts of his victims. The odontologist was able to prove that the *TOOL MARKS* on one victim were made by Ted Bundy's teeth.

Bite marks are often part of violent crimes such as sexual assault, sexual homicide, and child abuse. Specialists categorize such crimes as "anger-impulsive," a spur-of-the moment act; "sadistic," characterized by protracted biting; and "ego cannibalistic," where the killer symbolically consumes the victim. As Richard A. Walter, M.D., said in "An Examination of the Psychological Aspects of Bite Marks," in the March 1984 issue of the *American Journal of Forensic Medicine and Pathology,* "Meeting challenges of every perceived threat of their virility, mastery and dominance, the biter's aim is to obliterate the body, absorb the soul, and wear the enemy's strength." Bite marks are often of the sucking type, long and drawn out as opposed to a quick, tearing action.

bite suit

Protective suit worn by a trainer of police attack dogs.

bite work

The portion of a police dog's training during which it is taught to bite.

black and white

A police car.

Police tend to characterize their patrol cars by colors. For example, the Los Angeles PD, which has black-and-white cars, call them black and whites, whereas New York City police call theirs blue and whites.

Police cars are usually painted in distinctive colors so there's less chance of them being misidentified, particularly during a chaotic situation. The distinctive identifying marks also serve as a crime deterrent. If someone with a felony in mind sees a police car in the area, he or she might think twice before proceeding. One trick traffic cops pull is to park an empty police car by the side of the highway. The sight of it does wonders to slow speeders down.

black hole

A prison nickname for disciplinary segregation.

Sometimes it is simply called the *hole,* but it refers to a special cell within a prison where particularly unruly or defiant convicts— or those who have broken prison rules—are sent to be punished and isolated.

The severity of the black hole depends on the prison, but there is no question about how horrendous the place was that fathered the term. The Black Hole was a name given to a tiny cell in Fort Williams, a prison in Calcutta, India. In 1756, 146 men were jammed into the Black Hole for an entire night; by morning, only 23 were still alive.

See also *BOX* and *CELL.*

Black Talons

Brand name for a popular second generation of *HOLLOW POINT BULLETS.*

Destructive technology has been much improved in these bullets. The point on an original hollow point bullet slightly deforms on impact. With Black Talons, the point as well as the metal casing peels back to form a *shuriken* (Japanese for "throwing star"), says the magazine *Handguns for Sports and Defense. Gun Digest* characterizes the Black Talon as "very nasty, very effective, the one by which all other modern high-performance bullets are judged."

Black Talons, which are made by Winchester, are the most notorious of hollow point bullets and inflict devastating wounds. As of December 1993, Black Talons had been pulled from the market in response to a threat from Senator Daniel Patrick Moynihan of New York to raise the tax on them 10,000 percent. Other brands of hollow point bullets are Remington's Golden Saber and PMC's Starfire. The bullets currently cost about $2 each.

See also *DUMDUMS.*

black tar

A slang name for heroin imported from Mexico.

This heroin gets its name from its tarlike appearance; it may also be sticky and rootlike in appearance. The color varies from dark brown to black.

Black tar is a very crude form of heroin that is sold on the street in quantities that are 40 percent to 80 percent pure. Sometimes it is diluted with burnt cornstarch; sometimes the tar is converted into a powder to which conventional diluents, such as mannitol or quinine, are added. It is usually taken by injection.

Black tar is popular in the western United States.

blanks

Low-quality drugs.

Drug buyers have no way of telling the quality or purity of the drugs they purchase on the street, except by the reputation of the dealer selling the drug.

A regulated drug undergoes an average of ten years' testing by the U.S. government before being licensed for sale. Unregulated drugs require nothing.

Other names for low-quality drugs are *lemonade* and *Lipton tea*.

blitz rape

An unexpected sexual assault committed by a stranger.

It is one of the terms coined by Ann Burgess and Lynda Holmstrom in their studies at Beth Israel Hospital in Boston of rape victims in the early 1970s. When women think of rape, it is the unexpected assault that most often comes to mind and is most feared because of the level of violence with which it is associated.

"Blitz" is a German word that means "lightning."

blizzard

A cluster of traffic summonses issued to one driver all at once.

Also called a *package* of summonses. Officers say that whether someone gets tickets—and how many—can depend to some degree on the attitude projected by the driver. "If the driver's snotty," says one officer, "you drop the hammer. If he's not, you might just let him drive away."

And of course most drivers are vulnerable to getting a blizzard of tickets, because at any given time most if not all cars are in technical violation of some traffic law, such as driving with slightly worn tires. Sometimes the driver has committed other offenses

17

besides the one he or she was stopped for; in such case, the traffic officer applies the law rigidly.

blood

A black American male.

The origin of the term is not known definitively, but it may derive from "blood brother." Separately, both words are commonly used among black males.

Bloods

Los Angeles gang.

blow

1. Cocaine.
2. Inhale cocaine.

"Blowing" is a quick way to get drugs working in one's system. A line of cocaine is carefully set up on a smooth surface. Then, using rolled-up currency or something similar, it is inhaled. Within ten seconds the user will feel the effect.

While fast, inhaling cocaine routinely damages the delicate membranes of the nose, producing an affliction known as *RAT'S NOSE,* and eventually ruptures them. Over time, drug inhalation can cause a hole inside the nose.

Other terms for inhaling cocaine are blow blue, blow coke, blow smoke, cork the air, do a line, geeze, hitch up the reindeers, go on a sleigh ride, horn, horning, one and one, pop, sniff, snort, sporting, toke and toot.

See also *COKE.*

blow away

Kill.

In recent years this has been a popular term for killing some-one, usually by gun. Like *SMOKE,* it stems from the image of the victim disappearing.

blown cover

To have an *UNDERCOVER* or hidden identity discovered.

Spy novels and police literature contain numerous references to covers being blown. When it happens, it can be quite hazardous for the officer. Criminals who normally wouldn't think of killing a law enforcement officer act on the spur of the moment, only thinking of the consequences when it's too late.

blue flu

A group of police officers feigning illness.

This term got its start with the New York City Police Department in the 1960s when a significant number of police officers failed to show up for work, claiming they had the flu when in fact few if any were ill. They were protesting the way they thought the city was treating them. The law does not allow police officers to strike, so this became their means of protest.

blue ribbon jury

See *GRAND JURY*.

blue wall

Police togetherness.

Blue is the most common color of police uniforms, and the term describes the psychological and symbolic drawing together of the police against any perceived enemy, such as criminals in general, an investigative review board, or the media. The source of this togetherness is survival: Cops depend on each other every day for years to stay alive. "When you drive up to a liquor store," said one cop, "and you know a heist is going down, and the guy beside you is the only friend you have, you build togetherness."

This bond is extremely powerful, so much so that many cops will look the other way when one of their own is corrupt. Indeed, the greatest sin one cop can commit against another is betrayal. A police officer who betrays another is perceived by most other cops as despicable. Frank Serpico is a prime example of this. He testified against fellow cops in the Knapp Commission Hearings on Corruption in the NYPD in the 1960s, and from that moment on was verboten. When he was shot in the face in a drug raid subsequent to his testimony, it was suspected that he had been shot by another cop. Today one name for an untrustworthy cop is *a Serpico.*

See also *CIVILIANS*.

blunt

A hollowed-out cigar that is filled with marijuana.

A blunt allows someone to smoke marijuana but disguise its smell with cigar tobacco. The term stems from the use of Phillies Blunts, a cheap, fat cigar that was found to be ideal for the purpose.

blunt-force injuries

Injuries usually characterized by outward signs of lacerations and bruising and caused by a *BLUNT INSTRUMENT.*

Blunt-force injuries are normally delivered to the head and produce external signs of attack, but this is not an absolute. A person may receive a severe head injury and appear to be fine but may die later of internal bleeding. Sidney Weinberg, medical examiner for Suffolk County, New York, once examined a deceased man who had been hit in the head but seemed totally intact; autopsy revealed that the blow had turned the brain to virtual jelly.

Blunt-force injuries on the side of the head are usually more likely to be lethal than those on the front. Blunt force applied to areas other than the head can also be fatal. Injuries to the abdomen and pelvic area can cause internal bleeding. Bones may be cracked and pierce organs; such injuries may also be useful in determining which direction the force came from.

blunt instrument

Weapon that has no sharp edges and produces *BLUNT-FORCE INJURIES.*

This term is an excellent example of police terminology at its euphemistic best. If someone were hit on the head with a ballpeen hammer, police would characterize the attack as being made with a blunt instrument. A wide variety of items, from frying pans to candelabras, have been used in blunt-instrument attacks. By far the most inventive blunt instrument was created by writer Roald Dahl in a short story, "Lamb to the Slaughter," in which a woman beat her husband to death with a frozen leg of lamb. When the detectives came to investigate, she convinced them to stay and have dinner, and of course she served them the blunt instrument. They ate the murder weapon.

body armor

See *BULLETPROOF VEST.*

body bag

The bag used to transport the deceased from the scene of death to the morgue; also called a disaster bag.

Years ago bodies were transported in wagon baskets, but today the procedure is normally to wrap a corpse in a sheet so it can be lifted and then placed in the leakproof bag, which is then zipped closed.

boiler room

A bare-bones room with desk, chairs, and telephones from which *CON MEN* sell all kinds of fraudulent items from stock and land to chimney cleaning.

Such operations are often difficult to derail because they are run by savvy thieves who are aware of the law and hide behind phony identities and corporations. If the police move in, the company's lawyers are there to meet them, while the principals of the firm often move away to greener pastures.

See also *THE WILLIAMSONS.*

bomber

Someone who constructs and plants bombs in violation of criminal law.

Members of *BOMB SQUADS* say that people who make bombs usually make simple ones and that the simple technology and materials needed to make a bomb are easily available. For example, fertilizer was used as the core of the bomb that destroyed the Federal Building in Oklahoma City. Bombs can also be complicated and may well be the handiwork of a bomber determined to outwit any bomb squad that seeks to defuse the device.

Bombers send bombs for many reasons. Sometimes it's a warning message—the bomb is placed where it is not likely to kill anyone when it goes off. Some are sent for simple revenge. The most horrendous kind, those placed where many people are going to be gathered (such as an airplane or building), are usually the work of terrorist groups. Undoubtedly, the worst example of an airplane bombing was that of the Pan Am flight that exploded over Lockerbie, Scotland. Hundreds of people were killed, all innocent civilians. That bomb was very sophisticated, having been on the plane some eight hours before it was detonated.

Sometimes the bomber's motive is greed, killing someone for insurance or inheritance. Probably the most infamous example of this occurred on November 1, 1955, when Jack Gilbert Graham placed twenty-five sticks of dynamite on a plane leaving Denver and carrying his mother. The aircraft exploded in mid flight, killing all forty-four people aboard. Graham was ultimately captured and executed.

See also *BOMB SQUAD, PIPE BOMB,* and *UNABOMBER.*

bomb dog

A type of *SNIFFER DOG* used by the Bureau of Alcohol, Tobacco and Firearms (BATF) and other law enforcement agencies to sniff out explosive devices.

The BATF characterizes such an animal, in typical governmentese, as an "explosives detection canine."

bomb, pipe

See *PIPE BOMB.*

bomb squad

Police unit trained and equipped to deal with explosive devices.

bone orchard

See *BONEYARD.*

boneyard

A cemetery.

Technically, a boneyard is a place where the bones of slaughtered animals are stored for later use, such as for making soap, or where animals go to die. In 1902 W. J. Long said in *Beasts of the Field,* "I have met men . . . who speak of boneyards which they have discovered. . . . [T]hey say the caribou go there to die."

The term eventually came to refer to a human cemetery. Also referred to as a *bone orchard.*

book

1. To arrest and charge a suspect with a criminal complaint.

   Many police departments commonly use a large book to record relevant information; hence the origin of the term.

   Though *book* has always been a staple term in detective and mystery yarns, it was Steve McGarett, the main character in the TV show *Hawaii Five-O,* who etched this word into the public consciousness. At the end of every episode, which would invariably feature the arrest of the bad guy, McGarett would exhort his detective sidekick Danno with three words: "Book 'em, Danno."

   This term has been around since at least 1841 when a reference appeared in a book called *Fistiana:* "The names of individuals of distinction were 'booked' for indictment, should the prosecution of the principles…end in a conviction."

2. Someone who takes illegal gambling wagers. Also known as a "bookie."

boost

1. To steal.

   Boost typically means "to lift" and has come to refer to stealing, particularly shoplifting.

   There are a number of references to this term after the turn of the century. In 1915 W. Healy said in *Individual Delinquents,* "He was a booster himself, he had already stolen. He says: 'You come on, I know a place where we can boost.' "

   See also *BOOSTER BOX.*

2. A shill, someone who leads people to a crooked card game or other illegal enterprise with one purpose: to separate the victims from their money.

3. To inject a drug.

   See also *MAINLINE.*

boost and shoot

Steal to support a drug habit.

The drug user first steals, or boosts, the money to buy drugs, then shoots up.

booster box

A special box shoplifters use, placed over the item to be stolen.

The box has an internal mechanism that allows it to pick up an item so it can be carried out of the store without being detected.

See also *BOOST.*

border rats

Customs and DEA agents who work the Mexican border.

boss

A person in charge.

Police commonly refer to their superiors—whether a sergeant or a chief—as boss.

Mafia families also have bosses, including the one boss over everyone, *CAPO DI TUTTI DI CAPPI* (boss of all bosses).

boulder

Twenty dollars' worth of *CRACK.*

This common unit of sale refers to the size of the "rock."

bounty hunter

1. A person who tracks down *FELONS* for reward money.

    Those who do this for a living do it at their own peril, fiscal and physical. Bounty hunters are normally hired by bail bondsmen to track down clients who have *SKIPPED,* thereby putting the bail bondsmen at risk of losing bail put up for the person. Bounty hunters must register with the PD in whose jurisdiction they operate, and they may carry licensed firearms. They usually pay their own expenses; and should they bring the felon back, they get a percentage of the money they save their client.

2. A police officer who focuses on making arrests.

    Officers who want to can make a lot of arrests, but not all of their arrests can be characterized as quality arrests. Arrests for such infractions as having the wrong license plates or carrying a nunchaku are technically classed as *FELONY* arrests but involve little or no risk to the officer. A large number of arrests look good on an officer's record and may require him to go to court and testify, thereby earning overtime pay.

box

In prison, a special, isolated cell for disciplinary segregation.
See also *BLACK HOLE* and *CELL*.

boxed

To be jailed.

braggin'

Talking about one's exploits as a gang member.
This term is commonly used in the Los Angeles area.

brain

See *GOLD SHIELD*.

breaking and entering

See *BURGLARY*.

break night

An all-night drug binge that lasts until daybreak.
See also *BENDER* and *RAVE*.

break out

To escape from prison.

brewery

See *FACTORY*.

brick

A kilo of marijuana.

bridge of sighs

A walkway between the courthouse and the old city prison in
Manhattan called the Tombs.

For years the Tombs was *the* New York City prison in Manhattan for holding prisoners prior to their being arraigned. Thousands of convicts took the trip along the enclosed walkway that connected the prison to the courthouse. And if the prisoner was not freed at the hearing, then he or she would have to travel back along the walkway, a melancholy trip made with more than a few sighs of sadness.

bro

A comrade; short for "brother."

This term is commonly used by black males to indicate respect, regard, and unity. The term is also used by blacks when referring to a non-black whom they regard with affection and respect.

Some police use the term in a disparaging way, for example, saying that a crime might have been the work of one of the brothers, meaning a black male. At other times no disrespect is intended; the term is simply used to *ID* the perpetrator as a black male.

broker

1. Someone who acts as a representative of buyers and sellers when large amounts of drugs are sold.
2. In *MONEY LAUNDERING,* intermediaries who unite major drug buyers *(TRAFFICKERS)* and launderers and negotiate contracts for laundering services.

brown shower

Defecating on a person for sexual stimulation.

Some *JOHNS* pay prostitutes to do this, and some homosexuals also engage in this activity.

Like other unusual sexual activities, police like to be aware of it—what it is, who might practice it, and why—because it could prove relevant in a later investigation.

BSU

Acronym for the Behavioral Science Unit of the FBI.

This unit, based in Quantico, Virginia, is dedicated primarily to the solving of bizarre and heinous crimes, such as those committed by a *SERIAL MURDERER, LUSTMURDERER,* or *SERIAL RAPIST.* It has world-class crime labs at its disposal, the most up-to-date equipment, and very knowledgeable agents. It assists local law enforcement groups, and may provide agents to assist in local investigations.

The BSU was featured in the movies *Manhunter* (about the hunt for a serial murderer named Francis Dolarhyde) and *The Silence of the Lambs* (featuring the infamous Dr. Hannibal Lecter).

buck

To shoot someone, usually in the head.

The term may arise from the bucking action that occurs when a body is struck by a bullet, or perhaps the sound of a gun discharging.

bug

1. A small electronic device placed in a hidden spot to surreptitiously record conversation in a defined area. Named for its tiny, unobtrusive appearance, in recent years bugs have played a potent role in bringing gangsters to justice who would not have been convicted otherwise. Indeed, bugs have played a role in seriously, perhaps fatally, damaging the Mafia itself. In 1990 two daring FBI agents succeeded in placing a bug in the base of a lamp near the dining room table of Paul Castellano, at the time a *CAPO DI TUTTI DI CAPPI* of the five New York Mafia families, and recorded numerous incriminating conversations. The FBI also succeeded in placing a bug in an apartment of John Gotti, ultimately resulting in the conviction of Gotti who had allegedly violently deposed Castellano (who was shot to death outside a restaurant in Manhattan).

   See also *PEN REGISTER, TAP, WIRE,* and *WIRE MAN.*

2. A prisoner who is very cold and has no empathy for anyone else.

   See also *COLD SHOT.*

bugged

To be covered with sores and abscesses from repeated use of unsterile needles to inject drugs; also known as *loused.*

bull

Police officer.

This term has been around since the 1800s. The term was originally used by hoboes and certain members of the underworld; by 1920 it was commonly used by everyone in the underworld.

The term likely arose not only from the Spanish gypsy slang *bul,* which means policeman, but also from the image of a large and aggressive animal.

See also *COP.*

bulldog

1. In prison, for one prisoner or group of prisoners to harass another individual.

   Bulldogging is the practice of cowboys wrestling calves to the ground by the horns. In the prison context, however, it probably means to attack like a bulldog—relentlessly.

   A prisoner who is being bulldogged is in a very bad situation. The individual is not only being harassed by one or more inmates but is under scrutiny by other prisoners. Unless the victim acts to deflect or defeat the harassers, other prisoners will start bulldogging him as well.

2. To criminally harass someone.

bulletproof vest

Protective vest worn by police to shield the chest area from bullets.

Popularly known as "body armor" among police officers, these protective vests are worn for good reason: Statistics show that police officers wearing vests have a much better chance of survival. When cops are shot fatally, almost 50 percent of the shots impact against the torso area of the body—exactly where the bulletproof vest is worn. What's more, 80 percent of police fatalities are a result of being shot with a bullet that is .38 caliber or less, calibers that a bulletproof vest can repel without a problem.

Today bulletproof vests are a far cry from what they used to be. For years they were composed of a blend of ceramics, metal, and glass-laminated inserts and were bulky and unwieldy as a result. Then along came Kevlar, a light, soft material that is, pound for pound, five times stronger than steel. It comes with various numbers of laminations, but according to details in *Street Survival*, a book on police survival tactics, most officers favor the 8- to 10-ply material.

One unsubstantiated myth is that once an officer dons a bullet-proof vest, he begins to feel like a superman and interposes himself into life-threatening scenarios he would not ordinarily get involved in. Statistically, cops without soft body armor are just as likely to get into hazardous situations as officers wearing vests.

See also *FLAK JACKET*.

bullets, hollow point

Bullets designed with a partially hollow front portion designed to expand on contact.

These are the most feared bullets on the street, because when they strike the body they expand into a jagged chunk of lead, destroying much more tissue and making a much larger wound than a solid, smooth-tipped bullet. Hollow points also stay in the body rather than passing through as ordinary bullets might.

Hollow point bullets have been manufactured since the mid–nineteenth century and were banned by the Geneva Convention for use in warfare because of their destructiveness. Currently, the most potent hollow point bullets are *BLACK TALONS*.

See also *DUMDUMS*.

bullpen

A common cell in a prison; usually, one large room where a group of prisoners will be kept until assigned individual cells. Also called a *HOLDING TANK*.

bum beef

A false accusation that results in a conviction.

See also *BEEF*.

bumper beeper

A small transmitter designed to be secretly secured to a vehicle so it can be followed.

Though called a bumper beeper, this device can be attached to any part of the underside of a car, either by straps or by strong alnico magnets. Once in place it emits regular electronic beeps that

29

are picked up by the receiving unit of a trailing car, which is thereby able to follow and tell the direction the *SUBJECT* vehicle is going, how fast, and the distance between it and the trailing vehicle. Most bumper beepers have a range of three to four miles.

The device came into public consciousness in the 1960s when it was used by James Bond in the motion picture *Goldfinger*. It was also part of a scene in *Thief,* a film starring James Caan. Chicago police followed the character played by Caan, who became aware of the bumper beeper, detached it from his own vehicle, and attached it to a bus heading for Milwaukee. The cops faithfully followed the bus.

bumper fractures

Bone breaks incurred when struck by a motor vehicle.

When a body is found lying on a road, investigators use various means of determining if it is a motor vehicle *FATAL*. Fractures in the legs indicate they were struck by the bumper of a vehicle.

See also *FRACTURE MATCH* and *HIT-AND-RUN*.

bump off

To murder someone.

This is an old term, going back to at least the 1920s. In *Me—Gangster,* Charles Francis Coe wrote: " 'That's a tough neighborhood,' the dick assured me. 'I used to walk a beat down there an' there's been many a night when only good sense kept me from being bumped.' "

bunco

A con game.

The term may stem from the Spanish word *banca,* a card game similar to *THREE-CARD MONTE*. It has been in use since the nineteenth century; a crime report in the July 6, 1875, issue of the *Chicago Tribune* said, "The fugitive is the same person who bunkoed a stranger of $75 recently."

Today many police departments still have *BUNKO SQUADS* to handle such swindles.

See also *FLIMFLAM* and *STEERER*.

bunko squads

Police units that investigate con games.

burglar

Person who commits a *BURGLARY.*

burglary

Unlawful entry into a building with the purpose of stealing from it.

Burglary is a *FELONY* that is particularly hard on its victims, especially in cases of residential burglary. Victims frequently compare the experience to rape, a violation where all one's possessions are invaded. Some burglars do disturb and invade all of the victim's possessions, whether their search for valuables requires it or not. Occasionally, burglars have gone so far as to defecate at the scene, usually on valuable items such as rugs or a dining room table, an act designed to cause shock, rage, and sometimes literal sickness in the resident. Police say burglars do this because they are both angry and nervous. They may also find such activities thrilling.

The term burglary has been around since at least the late thirteenth century, but its precise etymology is not known. It is also called *breaking and entering* and *B and E,* the perpetrator being a *B and E man.*

burking

Homicidal suffocation.

Back when cadavers were casually bought for medical experimentation, they brought a good price, and in Edinburgh, Scotland, in 1829 a man named William Burke was quite good at supplying them. The only problem was that he murdered people to create his supply. He and a confederate would get the victim drunk, then Burke would sit on the victim's chest while his partner held the person's nose and mouth closed. Result: a cadaver with no marks of foul play.

The method is still used today by crafty murderers who want to make a death appear natural.

burn

1. To have money or valuables stolen.
2. Death by electrocution.

     The term "burned" has been around since electric chairs were invented. The meaning comes from the physiological effect of a lot of electricity flowing through human flesh. Among other things, it causes extensive burns on the appendages.

     Also called *frying*. Author Stephen King has referred to it as "riding the lightning."
3. For a police officer to be recognized by the subject of a surveillance.

     Being identified by someone who's not supposed to spot you is an unnerving experience for a police officer. Being burned is particularly frustrating if you have invested a lot of time and effort in the surveillance.

burnout

1. Fatigue after using drugs.
2. A heavy abuser of drugs.
3. The collapse of veins from repeated drug injections, or permanent impairment from drug use.
4. Psychological collapse by police officers.

     This is most commonly experienced by cops involved in high-stress assignments, such as *UNDERCOVER*. It also very commonly occurs when an officer is forced to shoot and kill someone. Contrary to the image of the police officer reacting like *DIRTY HARRY*, officers often require psychological counseling before going back on the job.

     But the daily grind of police work can also be very stressful. Police are in a constant adversarial position, whether giving out traffic tickets or walking down a dark alley with gun drawn. The changing hours, not coming home when expected, and calls in the middle of the night can create chaos with an officer's home life. All these stress factors contribute to high alcoholism and divorce rates among police—and burnout. Many police departments have counselors to help police avoid burnout.

See also *GOING NATIVE*.

5. A dilapidated tenement building.

burn patterns

The patterns created by the path a fire travels.

One way to determine if a fire has been caused by arson is to observe the site and see where the fire actually burned. For example, investigators will look to see if fire is "low burning," meaning the fire started at floor level; if it is, then arson is immediately suspected. A fire will not normally be "low burning" unless an *ACCELERANT* was poured on the floor and ignited.

Another technique is to examine wood that's been burned. This can show how long the fire was actually burning and whether an accelerant was used.

See also *POUR PATTERNS* and *ALLIGATOR EFFECT*.

bust

An arrest.

Busts usually involve the arrest of one person, but police also refer to "busting" a location, which means raiding it and arresting whoever's present. The term may have originally been used by blacks. In 1938 an article in the *New Yorker* mentioned, " 'One whiff (of marijuana),' said Chappy, 'and we get a bust' ('Bust' is Harlem for a police raid.)."

Knock and *POP* are also common terms for an arrest.

See also *COLLAR, FALL, KEEPER,* and *PINCH.*

bust out

1. An escape from jail.
2. To lose all of one's money, usually through gambling.

bust-out joint

A gambling house designed to fleece the gamblers.

Here, "bust out" refers to going bust, monetarily speaking. The term has been around since the 1920s. Damon Runyon made reference to it in his 1938 book, *Take It Easy:* "I knew him when he was nothing but a steerer for a bust-out joint in West Forty-Third, a bust-out joint being a joint where they will cheat your eyeballs out at cards, and dice, and similar device."

Bust-out joints are still very much alive.

busywork

Routine repetitive work in a criminal investigation.

In many criminal investigations, much checking of records, such as merchandise receipts, and other repetitive work is required; it keeps police very busy but usually fails to reap concrete dividends. Sometimes, however, busywork pays big. For example, in the 1950s when the "Mad Bomber" terrorized New York City, checking of utility records turned up handwriting of an ex-employee that matched that on notes the bomber sent. It resulted in the apprehension, arrest, and conviction of George Metesky and ended the terror that had swept the city.

button man

A soldier in a *MAFIA* family.

Button men do the dirty work of the Mafia—collecting for loan sharks or from people paying extortion, acting as enforcers, bodyguards, runners—whatever they are ordered to do. The button man may or may not be a *MADE MAN* (one formally inducted into the Mafia) but is connected nonetheless. Button men are considered the low men on the Mafia totem pole but are highly regarded within the criminal community because of their Mafia affiliation. One said the term comes from the idea that a button man acting as a *HIT MAN* makes buttonholes, or bullet holes, in his victim.

buy

To purchase drugs.

There are many other ways of expressing this, including *get a gift* and *get through*.

See also *HIT.*

buy and bust

A *STING* set up by police where an *UNDERCOVER* officer poses as a customer or dealer, buys drugs, then *BUSTS* (arrests) the sellers.

This is hazardous and stressful duty. After a number of years of going undercover, or *UC,* many officers quit or risk suffering *BURNOUT.*

C

Cadillac

A 1-ounce unit of drugs.

Also known as a "cad."

call girl

A prostitute whose dates are arranged primarily via telephone.

Call girls differ from *STREETWALKERS* in a number of ways, chiefly that they don't walk the streets looking for *JOHNS*, or clients. Assignations are made on the phone, and many clients come through recommendations or an escort service. Rates for call girls are also generally higher than those charged by streetwalkers; some may charge $100 an hour, others $500. Call girls also differ in that they will generally practice the more exotic forms of sex, such as *B & D*.

Some call girls work full time (four or five hours a night), and some are housewives who work only part-time to supplement the family income. Unlike streetwalkers, call girls often end their careers alive and well, and a few have been known to marry clients.

See also *GIRLFRIEND, GUMP, STREET GIRL, WORKING GIRL.*

can

1. Common slang word for jail.

Can goes back to at least 1912 when Donal Lowrie, an inmate at San Quentin from 1901 to 1911, wrote in *My Life in Prison,* "I was in the can ag'in, up against it f'r robbery."

The term today is normally used to describe the cell of someone who is serving a fairly short prison sentence. For example, if a man were doing life he would not be described as being "in the can doing life," but rather "He's in prison" or "He's in the pen."

See also *COOLER, JOINT,* and *PEN.*

2. One ounce of drugs.

canary

See *INFORMANT.*

canvass

To question potential witnesses at and around the scene of a crime.

Canvassing is standard procedure in a criminal investigation and is regarded as absolutely essential, perhaps the most important single activity in an investigation.

One officer put it this way in Mark Baker's *Cops: Their Lives in Their Own Words:* "A detective's major tool is his feet. His feet carry him on the endless journey of canvassing neighborhoods for witnesses. From door to door, upstairs and down, he knocks and identifies himself and asks his questions over and over again, hoping to come across the recluse insomniac who just happened to be gazing out the window at 4 A.M. when the crime took place."

Canvassing is not as simple as suggested in movies. It is hard, grueling work. At a typical murder scene an area with a radius of several miles is canvassed, and in many cases aerial photographs are taken. In addition, roads that potential witnesses may have travelled at the time of the commission of the crime are *ROADBLOCKED,* and drivers and occupants are queried as to what, if anything, they might have seen.

See also *GOYAKOD.*

capo

Short for *capo regima,* a captain in a *MAFIA* family.

capper

See *STEERER.*

capo di tutti di cappi

Italian for "boss of all bosses."

See also *BOSS*.

Carolina pancake

A mixture of lye and Crisco or bacon grease blended together and used as a weapon.

One cop spoke of a Carolina pancake in *Cops: Their Lives in Their Own Words* by Mark Baker: "What happened was that this guy was involved in a family fight and some cops showed up. He had made a Carolina pancake. A Carolina pancake is a mixture of lye, Crisco or bacon grease. Fat and lye. They cook it up and then they throw it on you. The lye will burn right through you. You mix lye with grease and you can't wash it off. It happens a lot."

carpet patrol

To search the floor for *CRACK* vials.

This is usually done by desperate crack addicts.

cartucho

A package of marijuana cigarettes.

casas de cambio

Currency exchanges in Latin American countries used by money launderers; can be either legitimate or criminal entities.

See also *MONEY LAUNDERING*.

case

1. To scrutinize a building to determine entrances, exits, and security in preparation for robbing it.

   There are many early references to case as preliminary work done by potential burglars. "To case" is usually attached to "the joint," as in "case the joint," an expression used by J. Edgar Hoover in his 1938 book *Persons in Hiding,* in which he wrote "when Ma cased a joint. . . ."

2. A court case.

   The term has been wildly popular in fiction and nonfiction book titles. One wonders what Erle Stanley Gardner, Perry Mason's creator, would have done without it.

3. A police case.

     The investigation of a criminal act.

cat burglar

A burglar with great physical skills.

Cat burglars can get into places that would frustrate ordinary thieves. They often use ropes and other equipment.

catch

To handle the investigation of a crime; usually used by detectives.

"Who's catching?" one cop might ask another. In most jurisdictions, detectives take cases as they come in; there is no attempt to assign a particular team to a particular crime. However, when a case is extraordinary, a commander may assign certain officers who are particularly good at solving that type of crime. Sometimes many officers will shelve their own cases and get involved; for example, if a cop is killed, an army of officers will be assigned to the case (and many will volunteer). The same holds true for a criminal abduction of a child, or a serial murderer or serial rapist.

catch a stack

To rob someone who turns out to have a lot of money.

cell

1. A prison cell.

     Prison cells are much smaller than many people realize. The federal penitentiary in Marion, Illinois, an extremely secure prison that houses only the most serious offenders, has some of the smallest: If an average-size man were to lie down in a typical Marion cell and stretch his arms back over his head, his hands would touch the wall and his feet would touch the bars. If he spread his arms out to his sides, he would be able to touch both side walls.

     See also *CAN, COOLER, PEN,* and *HOUSE.*

2. To be imprisoned.

     "I celled for a couple o' years with old Darbsy—he was doin' life." (Josiah Flynt, *The Rise of Roderick Clowd*)

3. In espionage, a group of allied operatives.

chain of evidence

Evidence collected and catalogued in a homicide; also called *chain of custody*.

It is important for investigators of homicides to keep everything in logical, consistent order when establishing their cases. "The chain of evidence," wrote Carsten Stroud in *Close Pursuit,* "started from the moment the *FIRST OFFICER* arrived at the killing, and Kennedy had lost cases because the sequence of events or the evidential chain had been broken by inconsistent or careless entries." Ideally, a written record must be kept of everyone who handles evidence, and when.

chain of custody

See *CHAIN OF EVIDENCE.*

chain (on the)

A group of new prison inmate arrivals who are chained together.

chalk the site

To outline a corpse on the ground with chalk.

This is a standard procedure in a homicide investigation. Chalk outlines show not only where a body was located but also serve as markers that indicate where small bits of evidence, such as bullet casings and blood, were located.

But chalking must only be done *after* the crime scene photographs are taken; otherwise, says Vernon J. Geberth in *Practical Homicide Investigation,* the defense attorneys can maintain that the crime scene has been contaminated. Geberth uses another term that is not yet used universally but may well find its way into police lingo: "chalk fairy." One photo in his book is captioned: "Here you see the deceased lying in the position in which he was found. The crime scene photo may possibly be 'inadmissible.' While the first officers were securing the scene, a 'chalk fairy' suddenly had the irresistible impulse to draw chalk lines around the body."

chase

See *FREEBASE.*

check kiter

Someone who writes bad checks.

Check kiters run the gamut from the basically honest citizen trying to make ends meet to the calculating, trained thief who lives on kited checks.

Check kiting can also involve big-time sums of money. For example, in 1985, E. F. Hutton and Co., Inc., a stockbroking firm, pleaded guilty to federal charges that involved check kiting and was fined $2 million plus the cost of the government investigation ($750,000). In addition, they had to pay back $8 million that they had defrauded from banks. The government said the scheme had lasted from July 1980 to February 1982, a time when interest rates were very high. In one aspect of this scheme, Hutton managers would write checks for more money than they had on account, using money that in effect didn't exist—just like an ordinary individual would do.

The term "check kiting" probably derives from the action of a kite: It is up in the air temporarily before it comes to rest.

cherry

A new prisoner.

chickens

Young male prostitutes.

The term has had a long history, signifying something young, tender, and defenseless. Young male prostitutes are a part of the underbelly of most big cities, and they usually become prostitutes just to survive. They are more like *STREETWALKERS* than *CALL GIRLS* in that they stand on a corner in the *RED-LIGHT DISTRICT* and wait to be picked up; the procedure is repeated many times a night.

Like streetwalkers, a steady diet of illicit sex, fast food, drugs, and the stress of having to survive burns them out fairly quickly. Once they lose their looks, their street value is much lower—and the burnout process is accelerated. It is not surprising that they look years older than they are and that they die much younger than they should, particularly in this age of AIDS. And of course some have the misfortune to be murdered. *SERIAL MURDERER* John

Wayne Gacy, executed in May 1994, patrolled the red-light districts of Chicago, picking up young men whom he then tortured, killed, and buried—most under his house.

chicken hawk

A male homosexual who frequents young male prostitutes, or *CHICKENS*.

chip

1. When a homosexual prison inmate, pledged to one man, has an "adulterous" liaison with another.

   Chipping is viewed very severely by the cuckolded partner, and verbal or physical violence is virtually certain to occur.

   The origins of the term are foggy, but apparently it was originally used to describe a low-class prostitute, or someone who was promiscuous. The word may also have arisen from prostitutes whispering the word "cheap" to prospective customers, or from the fact that prostitutes working southwestern and Mexican brothels near gambling parlors were compensated in gambling chips, which they cashed in. The word also sounds like *chipie,* a French word for a shrewish woman.

2. Occasional drug use.

   Some people are able to use drugs without becoming *HOOKED,* just as some people can have an occasional cigarette and not get addicted. Still, addicts will tell you that it's dangerous to use drugs even occasionally if you are afraid of becoming addicted.

   Other terms for the practice are *joy popping* and *Pepsi habit.*

chopping wounds

Wounds caused by a heavy cutting tool.

A wound produced by a heavy cutter like an ax, machete, or cleaver results in not only a deep gaping wound but also structural damage to body parts in the path of the weapon.

chop shop

A place where stolen cars are dismantled and the parts sold.

The normal procedure in chop shops is to only cut up and sell parts—rear quarters, noses, doors—without *VIN* (vehicle identification numbers) on them.

The word chop refers to quick cutting, and of course quickness is desirable when at any moment police may come through the door.

CI

Confidential informer.

This is an FBI term that describes members of *THE MOB* who work as informers on the condition that they will not be asked to testify.

circumstantial evidence

Evidence that infers a person's guilt or innocence of a crime but does not establish it with solid proof.

For example, someone may have been spotted in the area of a murder victim's house at around the time of death; or police might find an object that belongs to a suspect at the scene; or a suspect has no explanation or alibi for a particular period of time. It may look bad, but it's not absolute proof. On the other hand, a great weight of circumstantial evidence has often resulted in a conviction.

See also *PHYSICAL EVIDENCE* and *TRACE MATERIAL*.

citywide

See *APB*.

civilians

From a police point of view, all persons who are not police officers.

Cops in various regions differ in various ways, but all police—even cops like Barney and Andy working in towns like Mayberry—regard noncops as civilians. Despite the close relationship that police have with the populace they serve, there always remains an emotional gulf.

See also *BLUE WALL*.

C.K.

Crip killer.

The *BLOODS* are a Los Angeles gang; their members commonly

use the term to describe themselves as they relate to their archrivals, the *CRIPS*.

claim

To state what gang you're in.

This team is used by gang members in Los Angeles when asking someone for their gang affiliation, which is often designated by neighborhood—for example, "What's your claim, bro?"

See also *'HOOD*.

clear

To dispose of a criminal *CASE*.

"Cleared" is the universal term in police departments for "We don't have to deal with it anymore." When a case is solved or disposed of in any other way, it's considered cleared. Clearing cases is very important to police as an indication that they are doing their jobs. Police departments periodically publish clearance figures that indicate the number of crimes that they've dealt with and cleared.

A clear is also known as a *solve* in some regions.

clear up

To stop using drugs.

clip

1. To steal something.

   Vanity Fair explained this use of the word in its March 1927 issue: "When a patron in a night club is 'clipped' he isn't punched, he's 'taken' or 'gypped' out of some currency or he's overcharged."

2. An organized crime murder.

clocker

A *DRUG DEALER*.

clockin' paper

To make money from selling drugs.

close tail

See *TAIL*.

cluckhead

Someone addicted to *CRACK*.

This Los Angeles gang term is used instead of crackhead; it probably describes just how gang members view people addicted to crack.

CMIR

Currency or Monetary Instrument Report.

These reports must be filed with the IRS by financial institutions when $10,000 or more is deposited at one time. *MONEY LAUNDERERS* work a variety of schemes to avoid doing this.

c-note

A $100 bill.

See also *GREEN STUFF.*

C.O.

Commanding officer.

C.O.D.

Collect On Death—a scam that involves collecting money for items supposedly ordered by a newly deceased person.

As rackets go, this is particularly nasty. Con men follow the obituary columns to see who has died, and then send an over-priced bible or other item to the address in the name of the deceased. If the bill is not paid right away, they hound the survivors for payment. Many people pay rather than go through this hassle, particularly during a period of mourning.

cocaine

See *COKE.*

coke

Short for cocaine, an addictive drug extracted from the leaves of a coca plant.

Coca is an agricultural crop that can be grown only in the proper climate. It is now raised primarily in Peru, Bolivia, and Colombia.

A manufacturing process done in a *brewery* or *FACTORY* is needed to make usable cocaine. After harvest, the leaves are dried and then made into a paste called *opozo*. The paste is processed by skilled technicians into cocaine base; the base, in turn, is processed into cocaine hydrochloride or powdered cocaine by first adding other chemicals such as ethyl alcohol and hydrochloric acid and then filtering and drying it. This pure product is shipped to various countries where a distributor then cuts it with milk powder or the like before offering it for sale. Currently, powdered cocaine costs an astonishing $36,000 to $136,000 per pound. In powder form, cocaine is meant to be snorted.

Cocaine has many street names, depending on the area of the country where it is sold. Here's a roundup.

all-America drug	C-dust
Angie	C-game
Aunt Nora	cabello
barbs	caine
bazooka	California cornflakes
bazulco	came
Bernice	candy
Bernie	candy C
Bernie's flakes	carnie
Bernie's gold dust	Carrie
bush	Carrie Nation
big bloke	Charlie
big C	chippy
big flake	cholly
big rush	coca
Billie hoke	coconut
birdie powder	cola
blotter	Corrinne
Bolivian marching powder	cotton brothers (cocaine,
bouncing powder	heroin, and marijuana)
bubble gum	crystal
burese	dama blanca
burnese	double bubble
C	dream

duct
dust
dynamite (cocaine mixed with
  heroin)
el diablo (cocaine, heroin, and
  marijuana)
flake
flamethrower (cigarette laced
  with cocaine and heroin)
Florida snow
foo-foo dust
foo-foo snow
foolish powder
freeze
Frisco special (LSD, cocaine,
  and heroin)
Frisco speedball (cocaine,
  heroin, and a dash of LSD)
friskie powder
gin
girl
girlfriend
glad stuff
gold dust
goofball (cocaine mixed with
  heroin)
H & C (heroin and cocaine)
happy dust
happy powder
happy trails
heaven dust
Henry VIII
her
hooter
hunter
ice
icing

Inca message
jam
jelly
joy powder
junk
king's habit
lady
lady caine
lady snow
leaf
line
love affair
mama coca
mayo
merk
mojo
mosquitos
movie star drug
mujer
nose candy
nose powder
nose stuff
number three
paradise
paradise white
perico
Peruvian flake
Peruvian lady
piece
pimp
polvo blanco
powder diamonds
press
quill
racehorse Charlie
Rene
ready rock

Roxanne
sandwich (two layers of cocaine with a layer of heroin as the filling)
scmeck
scorpion
Scottie
Serpico 21
she
snow
snowball (cocaine and heroin)
snow bird
snowcones
snow seals (cocaine and amphetamine)
snow white
society high
squirrel (PCP and marijuana sprinkled with cocaine and smoked)
stardust
Star-spangled powder
sugar
sweet stuff
T
tardust
teeth
thing
turkey
tutti-frutti (flavored cocaine developed by Brazilian gang)
white girl
white horse
white lady
white mosquito
white powder
whiz bang
wild cat
wings
witch
woolas (cigarettes laced with cocaine)
yeyo
zip

See also *BLOW*.

coke whore

See *BAG BRIDE*.

cold case squad

Homicide squad that tries to *CLEAR* homicides of long standing.

Homicide cops say that this squad periodically looks over old cases and tries to clear them, sometimes more with hunches than anything else. They also say that cases of long standing often have a better chance of being solved than when new because as years pass, tongues tend to loosen and witnesses might be more willing to talk than before.

When a new homicide investigator comes on the squad in Suffolk County, New York, detectives have him or her go over all the old cases because new eyes might have new insights. In one case, a new detective found that the method of killing the victim was so unusual (it involved the *PERP* manually tearing out the victim's organs) that he was immediately able to tie it to an assault case he had been involved in. The result was the apprehension and conviction of a killer twenty-five years after the murder was committed.

cold hit

A random, lucky search by police that results in the discovery of illegal drugs.

cold shot

An action by a prisoner that is cold and heartless and totally disregards the rights of others.

Such actions are usually done by sociopaths—people who have no sense of other peoples' rights—which may well describe many people in prison. These individuals are known as *BUGS*.

cold turkey

Abruptly stopping the use of drugs.

The term may derive from the cold, clammy feel of the skin during withdrawal, like a turkey that has been refrigerated.

collar

An arrest.

This term is nearly universal among city police, FBI agents, postal inspectors, you name it. In standard English it dates back to around 1300, and for centuries referred to a metal collar or band with a chain attached that would be secured to the neck of a criminal. By the second half of the nineteenth century, it had come to mean arrest. G. P. Burnham wrote in *U.S. Secret Service* (1872) that it meant to "Put the collar on, to arrest a criminal, and 'iron' him." Today cops characterize collars as being good or ordinary, depending on the quality of the arrest. The best kind is the "felony collar," an arrest for a serious crime.

See also *BAG, BUST, FALL,* and *KEEPER.*

Colombian necktie

A murder in which the victim's throat is cut and the tongue is pulled down through the opening to resemble a tie.

This gruesome practice is done by Colombian drug dealers, who normally reserve it for a *SNITCH*. Though everything is relative, the Colombians, along with *POSSES,* are generally regarded as the most brutal of all drug-dealing *GANGS*. Perhaps their reputation is most fearsome because it is well known that they will kill not only someone who has crossed them, but that person's family as well. In fact, that is an implicit threat when dealing with Colombians.

command

Any group of police officers and facilities under the leadership of one person.

committal

Involuntary institutionalization by authorities of someone with mental difficulties.

complainant

The person who files a criminal complaint to the police.

The term was first used in the play *Henry VII* in 1498. "The same compleynaunt, not provying the mater of his seid bill to be true."

complaint

A formal allegation against a person or persons.

The complaint is normally in writing except in homicides where it is implied: I've been murdered, and I want something done about it.

Police slang for a complaint is a *SQUEAL,* and the officer who handles it is a *SQUEAL MAN*.

See also *BEEF* and *BUM BEEF*.

con

1. Short for convict, a convicted criminal.

In 1893 J. Hawthorne wrote in *Confessions of a Convict,* "Prisoners are known as 'con' which is short for convict, and the whole body of prisoners is designated 'condom'—short for convictdom."

Con is by far the most common name used by prisoners and guards when referring to the convicted criminals. An *ex-con* is, of course, a former prisoner.

2. Short for confidence game, a dupe, or swindle.

All confidence games require one thing: that the victim, or *PIGEON,* have faith in the perpetrators of the con. If this belief is absent, so is the con.

See also *RIP-OFF.*

concealment

See *COVER.*

con man

A person who engages in confidence games.

See also *CON.*

connection

A drug source or dealer.

See also *HIT.*

consigliere

Chief counselor to the head of a *MAFIA* family; from the Italian *consiglio,* meaning advice or counsel.

Consigliere is a revered position in the Mafia; the man who holds it is regarded as very wise in the ways of the mob. Consiglieres tend to be older men.

contact high

A feeling of intoxication produced by inadvertently inhaling a drug being smoked by someone else.

See also *HIGH.*

contacts

General term police use for people who can help them achieve investigative goals.

Contacts can be inside or outside a police department and are extremely important to police officers. If an officer knows a *FED* or an *ADA* or even someone who works in the property room, for example, it could make a big difference in how thoroughly and quickly a case can be investigated.

contact wound

Wound that results when a gun is placed against a body and fired.

When a gun is fired at such close range, gases from the explosion burst between the skin and bone and make a ragged, dirty *ENTRANCE WOUND*. This wound is usually star-shaped or cross-shaped and is sometimes referred to as a stellate.

Some contact wounds are atypical in that the underlying organs allow gases to expand so there is no ragged entry wound. Instead, the entry is clean with a characteristic "muzzle stamp" or "brand"— the outline of the barrel hole and front site.

contain

To keep an unruly mob under control.

Law enforcement parallels military duty in many ways (uniforms, discipline, chain of command, armament, etc.), so it is not surprising that many military terms find their way into the law enforcement language. Contain is one such term.

contrecoup contusions

Bruising of the brain from a fatal fall.

Without an autopsy, it may be difficult to tell if a *DECEASED* is the victim of a homicidal assault with a *BLUNT INSTRUMENT,* which produces *BLUNT-FORCE INJURIES,* or a fall. The autopsy will clarify this. If the person has been murdered, the skull and brain will be contused on the side of the head that was struck. If a person dies from a fall, the contusions—which usually occur in the frontal and temporal lobes—occur in the brain directly opposite the point of impact. Reason: As the head strikes the surface, the brain is jarred loose and impacts against the skull on the opposite side. This medical insight has resulted in the conviction of many murderers who assume that there's no way anyone can tell if someone is hit with a hammer or jumps head first out of a window.

Contrecoup is a French term meaning "against the flow."

cooler

1. Prison.

    Cooler has referred to prison since at least 1884 when, according to the *Oxford English Dictionary,* Milnor Tellor said, "Arrested on the charge of drunkenness, lodged in the cooler overnight, then fined $5 in the morning."

    See also *CELL.*

2. Cigarette laced with a drug.

coop

A secret place where an on-duty cop stays when he should be working; also used as a verb to describe this practice.

"Cooping" is a common practice among cops. On cold winter nights when they should be on the *BEAT* checking store doors to see if they're locked, you may more than occasionally find them in a girlfriend's apartment, an all-night movie theater, a bar, or some other spot. Most cops have engaged in cooping at least once, so sergeants and other supervisory personnel may look the other way unless the practice becomes abusive.

Occasionally, cooping goes awry. One famous instance involved a New York City mounted cop who cooped himself and his horse in a boxcar, then fell asleep and ended up in upstate New York, where he had the unenviable task of calling his superiors to tell them that he was slightly off post—two hundred miles, to be exact.

This incident may well have served as the inspiration for this scene in Vincent Patrick's *The Pope of Greenwich Village:* A mounted cop takes his horse, Francis, onto a box car, falls asleep, and wakes up as the train is rattling across the New Jersey Meadowlands. While trying to force the horse to jump off, he draws his gun and threatens to shoot the beast. But Francis doesn't budge, and the cop ends up—in full uniform—having to call his boss from the Baltimore freight yards with an explanation.

cop

1. A police officer.

    This is perhaps the most common slang term used to describe police officers.

There is a widespread myth that both "cop" and "copper" derived from the copper buttons police wore on their uniforms years ago, but it came from neither buttons nor copper badges. It actually stems from the term "copper," an oblique reference to "copperstick," archaic slang for a policeman's truncheon. "Copper" was first used by criminals in the late 1800s to describe *INFORMANTS;* they later started using the word to describe a policeman. "Copper" was later shortened to "cop" and was gradually adopted by the general public. In the 1950s J. Edgar Hoover tried without success to stamp out public use of the term.

See also *BULL, FIVE-O, THE ONE,* and *THE MAN.*

2. To obtain drugs

3. To *PLEA BARGAIN.*

cop a plea

See *PLEA BARGAIN.*

cop bar

A bar frequented by police officers.

Many cop bars are owned by ex-cops, who of course have a built-in loyal clientele. It is said that many cops run successful bars because they know so much about them, having spent years on the other side of the bar both on and off duty.

A cop bar is a bad place for a *HEIST,* but this happened on at least one occasion. A man came into a crowded New York bar on a busy Friday night and pulled a gun on the bartender. It must have been disconcerting for the stickup man to be suddenly faced with the muzzles of a half-dozen guns.

In New York, cop bars are also known as *watering holes.*

count

A criminal charge.

The more counts a person is charged with, the more serious the situation for the accused. Often, however, a defendant may initially be charged with a raft of counts simply for *PLEA BARGAINING* purposes. In reality most of these counts are merely bargaining chips between the prosecution, who draws up the charges, and the defense. For example, a defendant may be charged with eighty-nine counts of various kinds of bank fraud, but in the end may be convicted of only three—the prosecution having lopped off eighty-six counts in return for a guilty plea.

coroner

The official in charge of determining the cause of suspicious deaths.

In some locales the coroner is the same as the *ME,* or medical examiner, and actually determines the cause of death. In other locales coroners are strictly political appointees who simply move the body to a funeral home. In those cases the coroner is not personally qualified to determine the cause of death, but hires a qualified pathologist to do so.

corpus delecti

The body of a murder victim.

Like a number of other law enforcement terms, this one is Latin and derives from Roman law. It originally meant the sum of the physical evidence that shows that a crime has been committed, but over time it came to refer to the body.

cover

Natural protection police officers hide behind when in danger.

People who specialize in survival tactics make a sharp distinction between cover and *concealment.* Concealment occurs when an officer is hidden from a suspect, but not protected against gunfire. For example, the officer may be hiding behind some cardboard boxes. If the suspect knows this, it would be very easy to simply riddle the boxes with gunfire and hit the officer.

Cover is something that hides all or most of the officer's body and can't be penetrated by bullets, such as a brick wall, a fire hydrant, or a street mailbox.

One of the great myths perpetrated by television and the movies is that an officer is protected when he hides behind a car door. In fact, this is no protection at all—even *.22* bullets will bore right through a car door's thin sheet metal.

cover story

A carefully crafted lie told by an undercover police officer or spy.

Cover stories are crafted in such a way that they are impossible to check, or if they're checked, they're found to be true.

coyote date

A pickup date who looks very undesirable "the morning after."

"You see policemen with coyote dates," one cop explains in Mark Baker's *Cops: Their Lives in Their Own Words*. "When you wake up in the morning and she's lying on your arm, you chew your arm off so she won't wake up as you leave. That's a coyote date. Who do you think a guy meets in topless bars and strip joints and hooker bars?"

The reference to the coyote is based on the well-documented fact that coyotes who are caught in traps will chew through the captured limb in order to escape.

CP

Command post.

The command post is the center of operations close to a crime scene.

CPL

Abbreviation for criminal procedure law.

crack

1. A concentrated smokable form of cocaine.

   Crack has been a most terrible addition to the array of addictive drugs, mainly because it is very cheap ($5 to $10 per vial, each containing several "rocks") and highly addictive.

   Crack, or crack cocaine, is produced when powdered cocaine is dissolved in water, combined with baking soda, and heated until the water evaporates, leaving crack rocks.

   The following is a list of street names for crack.

apple jacks
Js
bad
baby T
ball
base
bazooka
bebe
beam-me-up-Scottie (crack dipped in PCP)
beamer (crack smoker)
beemers
Bill Blass
bings
blowout
bobo
bolo
bomb
bomb squad (name of crew selling crack)
bonecrusher
bones
botray
bottles (crack vials)
boubou
boulder
brick
bubble gum
bullion
bump
caine
cap
Casper the ghost
caviar
chasing the dragon (crack mixed with heroin)
chemical
chewies
climax
cloud

cloud nine
crack back (crack and marijuana)
crib
croak (crack mixed with methamphetamine)
crunch & munch
devil's dandruff
dime
double yoke
eastside player
egg
eightball (crack mixed with heroin)
eyeopener
famous dimes
fat bags
fifty-one (crack sprinkled on tobacco)
fire (crack and methamphetamine)
fish scales
fries
fry daddy (marijuana joint laced with crack)
geek (crack mixed with marijuana)
gimme (joint laced with crack)
girl
gold
golfball
grit
groceries
hail
half track
hard line
hard rock
hamburger helper
hit
hotcakes
how ya like me now?

hubbas
I am back
ice cube
issues
kibbles-and-bits (crumbs of crack)
Kokomo
juice joint (crack laced with marijuana)
Johnson
moonrock (crack mixed with heroin)
nuggets
one-fifty-one (crack sprinkled on tobacco)
outerlimits (crack and LSD)
P-funk (crack mixed with PCP)
parachute (smokable crack and heroin mixture)
parlay
paste
pebbles
peewee
piece
piles
pony
primo
raw
ready rock
regular "P"
rock
rooster
Rox/Roxanne
Roz
schoolcraft
scramble
scruples

sherms
sightball
slab
sleet
smoke
space base (crack dipped in PCP)
space cadet (crack dipped in PCP)
space dust (crack dipped in PCP)
speed
square time Bob
stones
sugar block
swell up
tension
thirty-eight (crack sprinkled on marijuana)
top gun
torpedo (crack and marijuana)
tragic magic (crack dipped in PCP)
troop
turbo (crack and marijuana)
ultimate
wave
white ball
white ghost
white sugar
woolas (crack sprinkled on marijuana)
wrecking crew
yahoo/yeaho
Yale
yimyom

2. A spot in a *BEAT* or patrol area where police can safely park their cars.

crack house

Place where crack is sold or smoked.

Crack houses emerged in the 1980s when crack became *the* drug on the streets.

The houses differ. Some are like *SHOOTING GALLERIES* in the sense that users gather in them and share the equipment for smoking the crack. This type of house was characterized by Detroit law enforcement units as a "buy, get high, and party" type of house, with sex also part of the festivities.

Another type of crack house, also identified by Detroit authorities, is simply a place where the drug is sold. This is characterized as a "hole in the wall" type. The crack buyer slips money through a small opening in the door, and the drug is then passed out through the opening to the user, who leaves and uses the crack elsewhere.

The latter type of crack house often has reinforced doors, because dealers know that the doors may have to withstand an attempt by law enforcement agencies to batter them down. And if the authorities do get in, they may be met by a couple of pit bull terriers, dogs that drug dealers keep locked up in a closet and release if someone breaks in.

crash

1. Feeling of depression after the effects of a drug wear off.
2. Sleeping off the effect of a drug.

crew

An affiliated collection of criminals.

Police refer to a crew in the same sense that they refer to a gang or mob. In Chicago "The Crew" is a formal name used for the mob. In recent years a crew has also come to mean a gang comprised of young people.

crime scene

The place where a crime has occurred.

criminalistics

The use of the physical sciences in the detection of crime.

The term first emerged in America in 1949, coined by Mssrs. O'Hara and Osterburg who wrote in *Criminalistics: The Application of the Physical Sciences to the Detection of Crime,* "The authors have decided, for the purposes of the present text, to use the term criminalistics in referring to the work of the police laboratory. This is not entirely a neologism. The words Krimionalistic, criminalistique, and criminalistica are in common use in continental Europe."

Crips

Los Angeles gang.

cross-dresser

See *TRANSVESTITE.*

cruising

A search for sexual assignations, usually homosexual.

In a police context, this often refers to searching for same-sex prostitutes.

CSU

Crime scene unit.

Most big-city PDs have crime scene units whose job is to descend on a crime scene and collect and protect the evidence. Such units comprise a variety of specialists, some who collect fingerprints, others who take photographs, others who search for physical evidence.

To the ordinary person, a crime scene may not look like it could give up much usable evidence. Many people—including police officers—are blase about such things. Perhaps the worst example of this occurred at the Sharon Tate murder scene in Los Angeles. Investigators were excited when they discovered a bloody fingerprint on the front doorbell of the house. It turned out to be the fingerprint of a uniformed officer at the scene: He had touched a victim lying outside the house, gotten some blood on his fingers, and then blithely pressed the doorbell.

cube

Morphine.

cube head

Someone who takes excessive amounts of morphine.

cuff

To handcuff someone.

In law enforcement lingo, one often hears "Put the cuffs on him" or "Cuff 'em." The complete word—handcuffs—is seldom used.

Cuffing someone can be a very dangerous procedure because it puts the police officers in close physical contact with often desperate suspects. An experienced police officer never attempts to cuff a suspect alone and thus avoids the risk of losing control and being overpowered by the suspect. Many police officers have been injured or killed trying to cuff a suspect alone. Handcuffing is usually a two-person operation, with one officer handcuffing the suspect, while the other stands at the ready, gun drawn.

Standard procedure is to handcuff the right hand of a suspect first, because in 90 percent of the cases this is likely to be the dominant hand—and the biggest threat.

cut

To increase a drug's bulk and dilute its impact by adding milk powder (lactose) or some other substance.

Most drugs would not look like much if bought in pure form. For example, only about 5 percent of a bag of heroin is actually heroin; the rest is the material used to cut it.

Such cuttings are not performed in the most sanitary conditions, and many times drugs are contaminated with another substance. Nevertheless, most buyers are willing to take the risk.

CW

Confidential witness.

FBI term for an informer who goes undercover with the understanding that his or her identity may be disclosed later.

D

dart-out accident

An accident that occurs when a pedestrian unexpectedly "darts out" into the path of an oncoming car.

Children are usually the victims of dart-out accidents. Police investigators say that there's not much chance that a driver can avoid hitting someone in such a situation, but emotional reactions are typical: (1) The driver comes unglued, and (2) the parents of the child, or the person entrusted with the child's care, feel guilt at the child being involved in the accident and berate the driver—or worse. Mobster John Gotti's 10-year-old son, Anthony, darted out in front of a neighbor's car and was killed. There was no way the neighbor could have avoided hitting the boy, because he was driving toward Jamaica Bay and the glare from the water temporarily blinded him. Though traveling at a legal speed, he had no chance to see the child. A few weeks later witnesses observed Gotti's henchmen clustered around the driver beating him with baseball bats. He was never seen again.

DCDS

Abbreviation for "deceased confirmed dead at scene."

DEA

Drug Enforcement Administration.

It is the goal of this agency to control the selling of illegal drugs in the United States. The DEA works in tandem with a number of other agencies and has local police officers attached to it in certain key cities.

deadly force (use of)

The discharge of a firearm by a police officer in the course of doing his or her job.

The average street cop's job was once described by a longtime Detroit detective as being like that of an airline pilot's: "Long hours of endless boredom interrupted by moments of stark terror." Not all policemen experience these moments. The vast majority never remove their guns from their holsters except to clean them or fire them at a range.

But when officers do fire their weapon at a criminal, it is, as Vernon Geberth put it in *Practical Homicide Investigation,* an "awesome responsibility." Shooting someone can carry with it burdens that include civil and criminal litigation as well as severe psychological difficulties.

death fart

Gas expelled by a dead person.

When a person dies, gases accumulate and these gases are sometimes released. Police say the smell is much worse than normal flatulence. It is these gases, incidentally, that give a body buoyancy (see *FLOATER*) and enable it to rise to the surface of a body of water despite having great weight secured to it. Many criminals have underestimated what such gases can do: A criminal chains a car transmission around a victim and dumps it in a lake; a week later the body—with the transmission still secured—bobs to the surface.

death notification

The act of notifying the next of kin of the death of a loved one.

This is a very difficult job, and police are trained in how to do it. One cop who did it a lot explained that when he showed up at someone's door he always had his hat off. "They got the message right away, subliminally, that something was really wrong."

debug

To remove or render inoperative all concealed microphones, known as *BUGS,* from an area.

"When walls have ears, call a debugging man," said *Business Week* in its October 31, 1964, issue. If you do, be prepared to pay. Debugging an area was and is always expensive.

The Mafia, stunned by arrests and defections over the past few years, conducts its business differently now. In the Bergin Hunt and Fish Club, a place where John Gotti once held court and was considered safe, it is now forbidden to speak about company business inside the building; in fact, member names are not even allowed to be used.

Areas can be built that defy debugging. One way is to install chicken wire on the walls and ceilings. This wreaks havoc with the electronic signals being generated. For aesthetics, the chicken wire can be covered with wallboard or paneling.

decedent

See *DECEASED*.

deceased

A dead person.

Deceased is one standard term cops use to describe someone who is dead, whether the death is natural, suicide, or murder. Like many other police terms, it is also euphemistic, much less jarring than saying "dead person."

The *Oxford English Dictionary* speaks of its euphemistic quality: "In its origin a euphemism (L. *decessus fier mors*) and still slightly euphemistic or at least less harsh and realistic than death; it is the common term in legal and technical language where the legal or civil incidence of death is in question, without reference to the act of dying."

Deceased arose for the Latin term "to depart," itself a euphemism. *Decedent* is also used by many departments.

deck

One to 15 grams of heroin.

Heroin is commonly sold in this unit.

deep

Los Angeles gang lingo meaning many gang members; for example, "Yeah, those dudes roll deep."

deuce (a)
Two dollars' worth of drugs.

deuce (the)
The notorious area in New York City on 42nd Street between Sixth and Ninth Avenues in Manhattan.

In the last ten years or so, this area of Manhattan has changed greatly, being modernized and cleaned up, but it remains one of the sleaziest areas of the city.

dews
Ten dollars' worth of drugs.

defense wounds
The cuts, contusions, and abrasions found on the hands, wrists, and arms of homicide victims that were incurred during the struggle with the murderer.

When someone is attacked, the normal reaction is to use one's hands to defend against the assault; predictable wounds result. Defense wounds are important clues for homicide investigators who want to reconstruct how a person was murdered.

To throw the police off, a murderer who is knowledgeable about homicide investigation may try to make it appear as if a struggle took place. Homicide detectives are always alert to this tactic. "I'm not so sure these are legit defense cuts," one cop said to another in Carsten Stroud's *Close Pursuit*. "They look a little stagy. Too regular, y'know what I mean? Like they been arranged in neat little rows. Most of your defense cuts, they're all over the wrists and hands, every which way, this 'n that, y'know?"

designer drugs
Potent synthetic analgesics.

Although made illegally, the ingredients of these drugs are not illegal and therefore are not subject to federal regulation and monitoring. Few designer drugs have found a permanent market niche.

One group of designer drugs are the fentanyls. One of these, sold on the streets of Los Angeles under the name "China White" is thought to have caused many overdose deaths. Deaths occur because of impurities in the drugs, as well as the inexperience of users.

Some of the more popular designer drugs have been businessman's LSD, cat valium, China girl, 45-minute psychosis, Special K, TNT, and Tango and Cash.

detective

See *DICK*.

develop

In a police investigation, to follow up on facts that may lead to the solution of a particular crime.

Detectives speak of "developing leads"—following the facts to wherever they may go.

dick

A detective.

This term is common in some jurisdictions and unheard of in others. For instance, New York City detectives are not called dicks, but detectives in nearby Suffolk County are. The term's origins are not clear, but it appears to have some relationship to male genitalia. The term might have come—negative connotation attached—from Donkey Dick, a term commonly used for a jackass. Premier lexicographer Eric Partridge suggests it might have come from the word "derrick," a term for the gallows, dubbed after the famous hangman named Derrick in the seventeenth century.

Hugh Rawson in *Wicked Words* notes that a "Dickless Tracy" is a female detective, but this is not in wide use.

See also *GOLD SHIELD*.

dime

1. A ten-year prison sentence.

    One speaks of "doing a dime in Joliet." See also *NICKEL* and *BIT*.

2. Ten dollars' worth of *CRACK* cocaine.

dime bag

Ten dollars' worth of drugs.

This is a common unit of sale.

ding

A prison inmate who is mentally disturbed, or feigning it.

The term is likely a shortened version of dingbat, a word that first surfaced around the mid 1800s, when it referred to an alcoholic drink. As time went on, it acquired a variety of meanings (including one as a euphemism for private parts) and has come to refer to a bumbling, incompetent person.

dinosaur

1. A police officer who has been working on the police force for a long time.

   Usually, anyone with over fifteen years experience as a police officer is considered a dinosaur. Some officers in the Nassau County, New York, PD wear little dinosaur pins to indicate their longevity.

2. An older officer who won't change outmoded ways.

dip

A pickpocket.

This term is primarily used by *BUNKO SQUADS*. It likely derives from the physical action involved: The hand dips into the pocket and extracts the valuables.

In 1888 the St. Louis *Globe Democrat* reported an item that indicated that no one is immune from a skillful pickpocket: "A dip touched (stole) the Canadian Sheriff for his watch and massive chain while he was reading The Riot Act."

dirtbag

Someone of loathsome character.

Dirtbag, along with *MAGGOT, MUTT,* scumbag, and shitbird, is a favorite term that police use to describe people they don't like. Around the turn of the century, the word simply referred to someone who actually went around collecting dirt.

dirty

Adjective used to describe a police officer who accepts bribes.

Dirty is the worst thing one cop can say about another, because dirty behavior is in diametric opposition to what police are sworn to do—uphold the law. Although a dirty cop may disgust others, reporting a dirty cop is the exception rather than the rule because loyalties—that *BLUE WALL*—go deep.

See also *IAD, GRASSEATER, MEATEATER,* and *SERPICO.*

Dirty Harriet

In the Midwest, the female equivalent of *DIRTY HARRY.*

Dirty Harriets are much rarer than Dirty Harrys, but they do exist and are every bit as ruthless as their male counterparts.

Dirty Harry

A cop who is ruthless in accomplishing investigative goals.

Its origin is the movie of the same name, *Dirty Harry,* in which Clint Eastwood played a San Francisco cop named Harry Callahan who was constantly in trouble with superiors for his unorthodox methods.

The name has nothing to do with *DIRTY* in the sense of being corrupt. Dirty Harry was a number of things, but he wasn't dishonest.

dis

To disrespect someone.

This is a very serious breach of behavior among black males, particularly those in gangs, and it can easily result in a homicide.

disease

Drug of choice.

disorderlies

Individuals who violate public peace laws.

Disorderly conduct is only a *MISDEMEANOR,* not a serious crime, but one can be arrested for it. A person who is drunk and bellicose might resist arrest, which can elevate the level of seriousness. In some police departments, disorderly conduct is known as a "dis con."

disorganized lustmurderer

One of two types of *LUSTMURDERER.*

In 1980 the FBI started to characterize lustmurder, a murder in which the victim's body is mutilated, into two categories: disorganized and organized. To each was attributed certain characteristics that would be helpful in *PROFILING* (drawing a psychological portrait) the killer and therefore possibly be helpful in tracking him or her down.

Agents Robert R. Hazlewood and John Douglas of the *BSU* in Quantico, Virginia, wrote in the April 1980 issue of the *Federal Law Enforcement Bulletin,* "The disorganized (asocial) lustmurderer exhibits primary characteristics of societal aversion. This individual prefers his own company to that of others and would be typified as a loner. He experiences difficulty in negotiating interpersonal relationships and consequently feels rejected and lonely. He lacks the cunning of the social type (*ORGANIZED LUSTMURDERER*) and commits the crime in a frenzied . . . manner. The crime is likely to be committed in close proximity to his residence or place of employment, where he feels secure and more at ease."

If the crime scene and victim show the *MO* of a lustmurderer—the victim was killed in a frenzied fashion (e.g., stabbed repeatedly and at random)—investigators might suspect a disorganized type and would start to focus their search locally, looking for his or her home or place of business. Such killers are usually young, so that would narrow the search even more.

DNA

Short for deoxyribonucleic acid, a nucleic acid found in every cell in the body that carries the genetic codes that control the function and structure of every component of the body.

DNA technology is to crime investigation what the airplane was to travel: It has revolutionized it. When analyzed, DNA varies absolutely from one individual to the next. In a sense, it's like a genetic fingerprint. These genetic fingerprints are in every cell of the body and are therefore contained in blood, semen, and other material found at crime scenes. All that the "genetic engineer" needs to do is compare the DNA of the substance found with that of a suspect.

The accuracy of DNA is mind-boggling—almost 100 percent. It is becoming widely accepted by law enforcement agencies, particularly since the FBI has paid homage to it—they have a DNA lab in Quantico, Virginia.

DNA has already figured in a number of sensational convictions and acquittals. Even if a DNA sample such as blood or semen is old, its genetic makeup can be discovered. Many convictions have been overturned because of DNA analysis. Prison gates have opened for people who had been in prison for more than ten years when on DNA analysis of old evidence buried in a property room somewhere proved them innocent.

It should be noted that although the science is unimpeachable, attacks are often made on the expert who interprets the DNA analysis.

See also *PHYSICAL EVIDENCE* and *TRACE MATERIAL.*

do

To murder someone.

Among law enforcement personnel this is probably the single most common term for murder. At homicide crime scenes one will frequently hear police say, almost exclusively, that the deceased was "done."

It is also a term used by the Mafia, but they like to say "do a piece of work." Like a number of other terms used to describe murder, it is euphemistic.

"Do" is probably a shortened version of "do away with" or "do in."

DOA

Dead on arrival.

The abbreviation does not just mean dead on arrival at a hospital. It can also mean that the victim is dead when the police arrive at the crime scene. In that case, police are careful—or should be if they suspect a homicide—not to disrupt the crime scene, keeping it intact for homicide detectives. (*FIRST OFFICERS* at the scene often feel a need to do something, such as moving the body, and this is a hindrance rather than a help.)

This acronym came into and has stayed in the public conscious- ness because of the motion picture *DOA,* which first ran in 1950 and starred Edmond O'Brien. A second version of the film, also called *DOA,* starred Dennis Quaid and Meg Ryan and came out in 1988 and further etched the term in place.

do a joint

Smoke a marijuana cigarette.

This is one of the most common phrases for smoking marijuana, but there are many others—for example, blast, blast a joint, blast a roach, blast a stick, blow, burn one, Bogart a joint (wet the end so others won't smoke it), smoke dope, fire it up, get a gage up, hit, hit the hay, mow the grass, poke, pull the dragon, tea party.

See also *TOKE* and *UP AGAINST THE STEM*.

DOB

Date of birth.

Once the police have this information on a suspect, they can access additional information from their own records and those of other agencies.

dodge

A shifty trick, an artifice to deceive or elude.

Dodge is somewhat archaic but still in use. It is generally used in *CON* games, the essence of which many times is to show one thing and switch another. Dickens used it in *The Posthumous Papers of the Pickwick Club* (1837):

"It was all false, of course?"

"All sir," replied Mr. Weller, "reg'lar do, sir; artful dodge."

doin' the Houdini

Cutting up a body and discarding the pieces so the body can't be identified.

This term was popularized in the Hell's Kitchen area of Manhattan (West Forties) and possibly coined by the Westies, a notorious gang that was in flower in the 1970s and 1980s. The method actually came from Eddie Cumminsky, an ex-con, now deceased, who had spent his time in prison learning to be a butcher. When he got out, he brought his skills and ideas to the Westies. After killing someone, Cumminsky would butcher the person, pack the pieces in individual pieces of plastic (maybe), and dump the pieces in the river.

The most notorious example of doin' the Houdini occurred when Jimmy Coonan, the gang's leader, and others decided it was time for Ruby Stein, a big-time *LOAN SHARK* who was the *BANKER* for other loan sharks, to stop living. Coonan and others lured him into an empty West Side bar one morning, shot him to death, cut him up in a sink in the back of the bar, and threw the body parts in the river. But one section of Stein's body, his torso, did not get swept out to sea as Coonan had planned. The *ME* discovered a scar on the heart from a heart attack and was able to match this with an X-ray of Stein's heart.

This caused a furor among Stein's fellow mafiosi, and suspicion fell on Coonan, who was able to convince Paul Castellano, *CAPO DI TUTTI DI CAPPI* of the New York *MOB* at the time, that he wasn't involved. For his part, Coonan was enraged—and he vowed that next time he did the Houdini with someone, he would use a blender.

The Houdini of the phrase refers, of course, to the great Harry Houdini (stage name for Erik Weisz, 1874–1926), premier escape artist. The Westies used the term to mean "disappear." In 1926, for example, J. Fait in *Big House* says, "Don't do no Houdini, or we'll lay you out."

dollar

One hundred dollars' worth of drugs.

domestic

Short for domestic disturbance, an altercation among family members to which police are called.

Cops regard this as one of the most dangerous situations they can encounter because of the high intensity of emotion that domestic disturbances generate. In a matter of seconds, for example, a woman who has called police in response to an assault on her by her husband can turn on the police officers. Police also know that repeated calls to handle a specific domestic may well be a precursor to a homicide. "There is always a history of abuse," says one investigator, "and then the final abuse—murder."

Domestic disturbances were dramatically highlighted in the murder trial of O. J. Simpson. Police had been called to his home eight times by his wife (and then ex-wife) Nicole Brown Simpson. Insiders viewed those calls as a significant history of spousal abuse that could well mean that Simpson had the capacity to murder his ex-wife and anyone who happened to be with her.

domestic interference

When a child is abducted by a parent or other relative in a domestic altercation.

Domestic interference is by far the most common cause of missing children. It refers to cases in which one of the parents has "kidnapped" the child while in the midst of a custody dispute. Thousands of children are taken this way each year, and the matter is almost always resolved without any physical harm to the child.

dominatrix

A female who physically and psychologically dominates and abuses her partner in sadomasochistic sex games.

The term is well known in police sex crime units. Dominatrices are usually associated with prostitution, though this is not always the case. Many big cities have houses of prostitution that cater to clients who want such sex games, but many individuals practice this form of sex legally, as a matter of choice and without monetary recompense.

See also *B & D.*

don

The leader or top person in a *MAFIA* family.

Originally from the Latin *dominus,* meaning "master," this Italian title of respect is given to a powerful Mafia leader. The Italian *donno* literally means "lord."

donorcycles

Motorcycles.

This term is primarily used by accident investigators in the Midwest. Because motorcycles are so hazardous to ride, many drivers inadvertently end up donating their organs for medical use. In the typical *FATAL,* it is the head of the driver—despite the helmet— that is impacted most severely; the rest of the organs remain intact and usable.

dope

Any addictive drug.

This term comes from the fact that in one sense drugs make a person "dopey," or stupid, as indicated by this early reference: "The oldest of the trio," said the Kansas *Times & Star* in 1889, "an Irishman from County Cork, was very hilarious . . . the 'dope' made him 20 years younger and very pugnacious." (Different things make different people laugh.)

The Irishman was undoubtedly on *OPIUM*, because all written references to dope from that period refer to opium. Dope eventually came to describe other drugs that produced a similar intoxicating effect.

dope dealer

Someone who distributes and sells illegal drugs.

Dealers are the distributors of drugs who supply the *PUSHERS* who sell on the *STREET*.

Also called the *pound dealers, ounce dealers,* or *weight dealers.*

dope pusher

See *DRUG DEALER*.

do-rag

The tight head scarf worn by young people, usually blacks.

double bang

To double-cross, betray; used as both verb and noun.

double whammy

The loss of a man's wife and job in a short period of time; a frequent precursor to hostage taking.

The double loss "usually occurs within two weeks," says one Chicago police officer (in *Pure Cop* by Connie Fletcher) who deals with hostage takers. A man may come home to find that his wife has fled with his kids, his money, his property; the only thing she leaves behind is a note saying she's not coming back. This situation is bad, police say, but as bad as it is, the individual can always commiserate with friends on the job, relatives, etc., and his life is still stable to some degree. But when he also loses his job, then the underpinnings of his existence have been removed, he's been "double whammied," and he can turn into a highly volatile hostage taker. He might take one of his children as a ploy to get at his wife.

See *HOSTAGE TAKER*.

do time

Serve time in prison.

drive-by

The act of shooting at someone from a moving vehicle.

The drive-by is the main method gang members employ to kill each other. It is simple and relatively safe for the *SHOOTERS*. They just drive by—usually in a stolen vehicle-and the victim, who is on the sidewalk or in a yard, is a sitting duck.

Drive-by shootings got their start in the East Los Angeles area, which is infested with gangs. The local joke goes that the abiding gang philosophy is "First we shoot, then we talk."

Gang members occasionally call a drive-by a *RIDE,* to further disguise their intentions to uninformed listeners.

drive on

In prison, one inmate or group of inmates harassing another inmate to achieve some end.

drive work

The process of teaching a police dog to bite powerfully and coura-geously.

drop

1. In a kidnapping, the place where the ransom money is left.
2. To take *LSD.*

    The most common way to take LSD is to "drop" it onto the tongue.
3. To pass counterfeit money.
4. In espionage, the place where communications and money are left for pickup by agents.

drop a dime

To inform on someone to law enforcement authorities.

The term was born when phone calls cost a dime, but still describes the practice of informing on someone to the authorities, though the communication may be written or in person.

Anger is usually the main motive when someone drops a dime. The person perceives that they have been wronged by someone, and calls authorities to bring misery into the life of their adversary. But anger is not the only reason—some people do it to make money. There might be a reward outstanding; or they might call the IRS and turn in a tax evader, knowing that they will receive 10 percent of whatever the IRS gets.

Elimination of competition is another reason. If you are a high-ranking Mafioso and want to eliminate an equally high-ranking person, then just drop a dime to alert the authorities where to hunt for incriminating evidence.

Finally, there is the concerned and involved citizen, the heroic person who will drop a dime just because it's the right thing to do. This is very rare, though, even when someone's life is in danger.

drop gun

A cheap, untraceable handgun used by police.

Some police carry this to plant at a scene in case they get involved in shooting someone and can't justify their use of *DEADLY FORCE*. This is also called a *throw-down gun*, depending on locale.

drug dealer

One who sells drugs; also called *clocker, mother, missionary*, and *player*.

Drug dealer is the most frequently used term for the common seller of drugs.

See also *BAG MAN, BALLER,* and *BARNES MAN.*

dry dive

Committing suicide by jumping.

Yet another example of grisly cop humor, this term is popular with Chicago cops.

See also *JUMPER.*

dry floater

See *FLOATER*.

dry snitching

In prison, informing on someone within earshot.

dumdums

A type of *HOLLOW POINT BULLET* made in Dum Dum, a town and arsenal near Calcutta, India.

Dumdum bullets were first manufactured around the turn of the century. There is reference to them in the December 7, 1897, issue of *Westminster Gazette:* "The piper hero, Findlater, was wounded in the ankle with a Dum Dum bullet."

The bullets were controversial to say the least. They were made with a metal jacket but a soft core at the point that would expand on impact with the body and created a jagged projectile. Use of the dumdum has been classified as a war crime by a number of international conventions, including the Hague declaration of 1907.

The modern offspring of the dumdum are *BLACK TALONS*.

dusted

1. Murdered.

    The term probably comes from the biblical "ashes to ashes and dust to dust." But for years it has been a standard way to say that someone has been murdered. "He has been dusted off by Vanderbilt" (H. Asbury, *Sucker's Paradise,* 1938).

2. Lift fingerprints.

    One method of lifting fingerprints from a surface involves applying a special dust with a soft brush to otherwise invisible impressions left by fingertips. The dust, or powder, sticks to the impression and forms visible prints, which are photographed and then lifted with a sticky tape. The photos serve as a backup in case the tape method goes awry.

    See also *FINGERPRINTS*.

dying declaration

A statement by a dying victim of a homicide identifying the murderer.

A dying declaration is always something that homicide detectives are alert to, but for it to be admissible in court it must satisfy certain criteria: The person making the declaration must be rational and must believe that he or she is dying; there must be no hope of recovery; the guilty party must be named; details of how and why the victim is wounded must be provided; and the victim must, of course, die. If the victim lives, the statement is invalid.

Obtaining a dying declaration can be done by experienced officers, and once they have it they are instructed to write it down, if possible. A witness is also helpful, but not essential: If the dying declaration is given according to the guidelines above, it will be an extremely powerful weapon in court, as many killers have discovered.

E

easy score

    To obtain drugs easily.

eat

    To take a drug orally.

eat your .38

    Suicide by a policeman.

    The stress of the job can have a disastrous effect on a police officer who has a relatively fragile ego structure to begin with, and police suicides are all too frequent.

    The most common weapon used in police suicides is a gun, which is logical since guns are handy and effective. For years, the standard police-issue gun was a .38 revolver, and this was most often used as the suicide weapon. The most effective suicide method is to stick the gun barrel in one's mouth, angle the barrel up toward the brain, and pull the trigger. Hence the phrase "eat your .38."

    The phrase has been around for many years and describes suicide in general rather than specifically by gun.

EDP

    Emotionally disturbed person.

    This can be anyone who police perceive as emotionally disturbed, from a potential suicide to a hostage taker. To some degree all police are trained to handle situations involving EDPs and to contain such situations, if possible, until an officer who has been specifically trained to handle the problem can be called to the scene. Some jurisdictions call EDPs "mentally aided."

EMS

Emergency medical service.

Nonpolice units who respond to medical emergencies.

entrance wound

Hole made by a bullet as it enters the body.

The entrance wound made by a normal bullet (as opposed to a *HOLLOW POINT*) is a small round hole with little bleeding and an "abrasion collar," which is a circular perforation and blackening of the skin around the hole. It is usually smaller than an *EXIT WOUND.*

See also *CONTACT WOUND.*

entrapment

A legal concept that states that law enforcement officials cannot manipulate suspects to participate in situations where they are likely to commit crimes.

Many convictions have been overturned because it was determined that a suspect was entrapped.

essay

A person of Hispanic heritage, usually a gang member.

This is a term used in Los Angeles to describe Hispanic people, particularly gang members.

ESU

Emergency service unit—a special police unit designed to handle all types of emergency situations that ordinary police are not equipped to handle.

Tabloid TV often depicts ESU officers because they are often involved with life-and-death situations and are frequently at great personal risk. For instance, they deal with potential suicides, people who've gone berserk, and people who are trapped in various dangerous situations.

ex-con

See *CON.*

exit wound

Wound made by a bullet as it exits the body.

This wound is normally larger than the *ENTRANCE WOUND,* because on impact bullets tend to flatten and become misshapen, enlarging in diameter. *HOLLOW POINT BULLETS* make a much larger wound than normal bullets.

See also *CONTACT WOUND.*

eyeball

For highway patrolmen, to estimate vehicle speed without radar.

While officers are equipped with radar to catch speeders, many say that with the right amount of experience they don't need radar—they claim that they can tell within a mile or two how fast a car is going just by eyeballing it from the side of the road. Courts have long held that a police officer's visual estimate alone is enough to sustain the burden of proof in court.

One officer in Mark Baker's *Cops: Their Lives in Their Own Words* explains what happens: "They get to court. If the guy pleads Not Guilty, the cop has to testify. How long did you follow him? Was he caught on radar or not on radar? How fast was he driving?

"I followed him for a mile and a half. Over that distance I clocked him at speeds ranging from 62 to 68 miles an hour."

Cops say that some officers always testify the same way. So even if he doesn't have particulars on a case, he doesn't have to worry. He'll just repeat what he said at every other court hearing.

Eyeballing is also known as a "visual estimate."

eyeball witness

Someone who has witnessed a crime; also called *eyewitness.*

Such a person can be invaluable in court, because they have seen the crime committed. They can describe it in detail and make a convincing case against the *PERPETRATOR,* through it may not be invulnerable. A good attorney can usually cast doubt on it.

At a crime scene there may be more than one witness, and police will strive to separate them. Police want to make sure that each witness tells his or her own story, not one that has been modified after talking with other witnesses. Such talk can produce stories that are consistent—but wrong. In addition, if there are multiple witnesses, one who has a dominant personality may be able to force faulty observations on the others.

Police are very aware that a person claiming to be a witness may well be the *PERP*. Sometimes criminals think that approaching the police as a witness is a good way to hide their own guilt, or they like to "play" with police.

In any well-publicized crime, police will have to deal with the *RAY PEOPLE,* mentally disturbed people who will say that they saw everything or committed the crime themselves.

eyewitness

See *EYEBALL WITNESS.*

F

factory

Clandestine laboratory where drugs are packaged, diluted, and/or manufactured.

Factories have proliferated over the last twenty years. Drugs are easy to manufacture: Neither a great deal of skill nor a great deal of money is required to produce them; the overall risks, despite an occasional explosion and fire and the threat of discovery and arrest, are few; and the profits are enormous.

Most factories are set up to manufacture a single drug, though some produce a variety. Most are located in rural areas, but some are occasionally found in suburban or city settings. Large factories are usually in rented buildings and have large-scale production equipment to turn out thousands of doses of drugs. People who work in them are called "cooks"; they may be students, teachers, chemists, engineers, whoever.

In general, factories have produced two dozen kinds of controlled substances, including stimulants, depressants, and narcotics. In the last couple of years, the two most common types of factories are those used to produce methamphetamine and amphetamine. They also make *DESIGNER DRUGS.*

fade (the)

When a criminal leaves a situation because of a sense of danger.

When people on the street involved in criminal activity sense danger, they do "the fade."

People who have survived on the street a long time while engaging in criminal activities develop this sense, much as a prey animal has a survival sense regarding predators.

fall

To be arrested and sentenced to prison.

In Europe the term has been around since the mid–nineteenth century. In America it was defined in 1934 in *American Slang:* "Fall, *v.* to go to prison. *n.* a term in prison."

See also *BAG, BUST, COLLAR, KEEPER,* and *PINCH.*

fallen off a truck

A stolen item, something that is either hijacked, the product of a burglary, or bought *HOT.*

It is usually associated with the *MAFIA,* and from time to time one hears it or a version of it in popular media. In the movie *Married to the Mob,* for example, the wife of one mafioso tells him that she is tired of living the *MOB* lifestyle, where "everything we own fell off a truck."

fall guy

A person who takes the blame for a crime he or she did not commit.

The term carries with it the sense that the fall guy is a fool, a person easily duped into taking the blame. According to *American Speech* (1935), the sense of the word was originally one of a dolt who gets caught doing a crime because of his or her own ineptitude, but later it changed to mean someone who takes the *RAP* for others.

family man

A clean-living cop both on and off the job.

The cop lifestyle is conducive to a high divorce rate; many officers become alcoholics, and many get involved in extramarital affairs, so a family man is highly respected.

In general, the term implies that the man has a wife and children, but this may not necessarily be the case.

fatal

Motor vehicle accident involving death; sometimes simply called an MVA.

Traffic accident investigators say that 95 percent of all accidents (some investigators put it even higher) are caused by human error. Only rarely are they caused by a mechanical problem.

As death scenes go, a fatal can be quite gory, and officers viewing one for the first time may have difficulty getting through it. The only scene that is gorier than a fatal is an airline crash.

fatal funnel (the)

In survival tactics, imaginary lines that fan out funnel-like from a doorway into a room.

Those who teach survival tactics say that an officer standing in a doorway in the mouth of that funnel can be in grave danger. Shots can be fired from any point inside the funnel. Knowing this, the officer may need to take evasive action.

Father Mulcahy syndrome

A police response to an emergency situation that is based more on the movies than on proper training.

The term is primarily used in Chicago. Lieutenant John Kennedy, who headed the Chicago Hostage/Barricade Terrorist Unit, explained it in *Pure Cop* by Connie Fletcher:

"A lot of what people used to do is based on old Jimmy Cagney/Barry Fitzgerald movies. Before there was HBT training (the police) did what Hollywood told them to do. Police would think (in a hostage situation) What do I do? And what the police officer had seen in the movies would click in. 'Oh yeah,' I remember—Get a priest. Get the mother. Get the father. Put them all on the phone. Leave my gun outside. Go in. Exchange myself for the kid. All these things, which are the worst things in the world to do in a hostage situation, the things that got people killed, are what, traditionally, police would do."

See also *HOSTAGE TAKER*.

fat pill

A buttered roll.

feds

Agents of federal law enforcement agencies.

The first verifiable use of the term "feds" was in 1916 in *Door of Dread* by A. Stringer: "Seein' Kestner and yuh'd told me the Feds have ev'rything first, I give him the glassy eye."

felon

One who commits a *FELONY.*

felony

A very serious crime.

Crimes fall into two general categories: misdemeanors and felonies. Felonies are by far the more serious and include such crimes as murder, kidnapping, rape, assault, armed robbery, and burglary. Someone who commits a felony is characterized as a *FELON.*

The origin of the word is unclear, but according to *Oxford English Dictionary* the most probable source is the Latin word *fel gall,* "the original sense being one who, or something which, is full of bitterness (or venom, the two notions, as many linguistic facts show, being closely associated in the popular mind)." Such a poisoned individual—or felon—commits poisonous acts characterized as felonies. The word goes all the way back to the 1300s and has kept its poisonous sense intact up to current times.

In the minds of law enforcement officers, there is a big difference between felonies and misdemeanors. They speak of *FELONY STOPS* and *FELONY FLYERS,* and the scariest thing they can say to a suspect is that the crime he or she has committed is a felony.

See also *MISDEMEANOR.*

felony collar

See *COLLAR.*

felony flyers

In the New York area, sneakers on any young black male.

For years one of the leading sneakers in the country was PF Flyers. The term evolved from the bigoted notion that any young black male wearing sneakers was a *FELON.*

felony stop

When someone suspected of committing a *FELONY* is identified and confronted by police.

When the stop occurs (the suspect may be walking along a street or in a car), the assumption is that the *PERP* is armed and gunplay may occur.

See also *PEDESTRIAN STOP.*

fence

Someone who knowingly buys stolen goods for resale.

In order to make thievery profitable, someone must convert stolen goods into cash. This is done either by the thieves or by the fence.

The word has nothing to do with property boundaries; rather, it comes from the word "fen," which goes back to 1698 and is defined by Eric Partridge in his *Dictionary of the Underworld* as a thief.

field interrogation

See *PEDESTRIAN STOP.*

fiend the heads

To throw a chokehold on someone to render them helpless and easy to rob.

This is a term used among black criminals in New York. "Fiending" refers to the chokehold; "heads" are the people.

fifteen cents

Fifteen dollars' worth of drugs.

finger

To point at, name, or otherwise identify someone as the *PERPE-TRATOR* of a crime.

The two most common ways in which a criminal may be fingered are (1) to be pointed out in a *LINEUP* and (2) to be ID'd from a *MUG BOOK* or a photo lineup.

fingerprints

Images left by a finger when it touches something.

There are three types of fingerprints:

1. *Plastic.* The print made by a finger when pressed into a soft material such as putty, gum, or the glue on a postage stamp. These prints are visible to the naked eye.

2. *Visible.* The image formed by a finger on which there is a foreign substance such as soot, blood, or soil.

3. *Latents.* The natural secretions of the finger, mixed with dirt and grease, leave these invisible images on a smooth surface. The term goes back to at least 1923: "Several latents were left at the house which had been burglarized" (A. Larson, *Single Fingerprint System*).

See also *DUSTED.*

finger wave

The digital examination of a prison inmate's rectum in a search for contraband.

See also *KEISTER STASH* and *STRIP SEARCH.*

fink

An *INFORMANT,* usually someone planted inside an operation specifically for the purpose of informing against others.

As H. L. Mencken pointed out in *The American Language,* "Fink probably goes back to the Homestead Strike of 1892" (a nasty strike that occurred at the Carnegie Steel Company in Homestead, Pennsylvania). The Pinkerton Detective Agency, which was widely employed in those days to put down strikes, was involved in the Homestead Strike, and some people say that fink is rhyming slang for Pinkerton. Another theory has it that it comes from the German *finch,* which means *canary,* another word for informant.

Fink is about the worst thing the criminal community can call someone, though even nastier terms—"ratfink" and "ratfink bastard"—are often heard.

See also *INFORMANT.*

first officer

First policeman at the scene of a crime.

The first officer at the scene of the crime, particularly a homicide, has a heavy burden. He or she has to notify the proper people to get involved with the case, try to detain witnesses, and keep the scene intact, pristine. It is a difficult job, particularly if emotional relatives are about.

fish

1. A new inmate.

   Fish are at great risk of being sexually assaulted, so they either establish a relationship with someone who will protect them—a *JOCKER*—or they fight back if they can. One fish explained his attitude when he entered a prison in Virginia: "When someone approached me," he said, "I hit them over the head with a pipe. You gotta send a message."

   There are extensive parallels between new inmates and fish. They are first put in a *HOLDING TANK* and from there they're on their own. ". . . New fish who do not learn immediately how to swim will undergo a devastating initiation rite (i.e., rape)," say Inez Cardozo-Freeman and Eugene P. Delorme in *The Joint Language and Culture in a Maximum Security Prison* (1984).

   Fish has been used as a slang expression in a variety of ways, mostly to express contempt (queer fish, cold fish, odd fish, etc.), but for a long time has also been used to describe someone who is inexperienced, a prime candidate to be *HOOKED*.

2. Victim of a *CON* game.

fish cop

A new prison guard.

Just as a *FISH* convict will be tested by other convicts, so too will a new guard. Convicts will confront him or her, and if weakness is shown, it will be exploited.

five-cent bag

See *NICKEL BAG*.

five-dollar bag

Fifty dollars' worth of drugs.

five-o

The police.

This *STREET* term comes from the popular crime show *Hawaii Five-O,* which ran on CBS in the early 1970s and starred Jack Lord as Steve McGarrett and James McArthur as Danno. With so many cop shows to draw from, it is impossible to determine why *Five-O* came to represent the police, though it might be because the character played by Lord was a hard-nosed, no-nonsense type and hard on criminals, which perhaps fits the image the average person on the street has of the police.

See also *COP.*

fix

1. To take an illegal drug, usually through injection.

    Fix is probably the single most common term used to express injection of a drug, most likely because it accurately describes what an addict needs most—something to fix the sick feeling that occurs as the drug wears off.

    In 1867, if you wanted to make yourself feel good, you drank a shot of liquor—"Claret-cobbler, eye-opener, fix-ups or any other Yankee deception in the shape of liquor" (W. H. Dixon, *New American*). It was still that way when reported in Flynn's magazine in 1934, but by 1936 it had developed into its present meaning: "Fix-up, a ration of dope, especially one that has just been taken" (American Speech, XI).

    Fix is also used as a noun to describe the act of taking in the drug, for example, "He needs a fix."

2. To influence actions or the outcome of events by illegal means.

    Fix in this sense usually involves bribes, intimidation, blackmail, etc. The word "fix" in standard English originated in the fifteenth century and referred to the act of repairing something, making it right or stable. The word began to refer to illegal acts near the end of the nineteenth century. Someone who fixes things in this illicit sense is called a "fixer."

    One of the all-time best fixer lines occurred in the movie *The*

Godfather, when the character of Don Corleone instructed his counsellor, or *CONSIGLIERE,* to make a movie mogul "an offer he couldn't refuse." The mogul did refuse it, but when he awakened one morning with his racehorse's million-dollar head in bed with him, he changed his mind.

fixer

1. In New York City, a location where there is a patrolman on duty permanently, usually in a booth.

    Most fixers are booths found in front of foreign embassies.

2. Someone who fixes things, in the illegal sense of the word. See *FIX.*

flak jacket

A bulletproof vest made from Kevlar.

Kevlar, produced by Du Pont, is five times stronger than steel. The term originated in the military: Flak is flying metal, the shrapnel from exploding shells. Military personnel wore these jackets to protect themselves from it.

See also *BULLETPROOF VEST.*

flash

1. Intentionally exposing one's genitalia in public.
2. Undercover agent showing money to drug sellers.

The word flash implies that something is done speedily. That is likely the origin of the term in this criminal sense because the action is usually quick.

Flash has been used to describe this action since the late 1800s. In 1896 writers John Farmer and Henley cited "meat-flashing" in the book *Slang V* as "exposure of a person." A person who does this is often characterized by police as being an *EDP* (emotionally disturbed person).

Flashing is not as common as it once was, at least in the sense of it being calculated, such as New York City's famed subway flasher of the 1950s, who used to wear a large coat, then sidle up to a train window where a woman was sitting, and open his coat as the train pulled out of the station. Still fairly common is the individual who will expose himself or herself while drunk or high on drugs.

flasher

One who flashes; see *FLASH*.

flashlight roll

A police technique of rolling a flashlight across the doorway of a dark room to illuminate the interior.

High on the list of hazardous situations for a police officer is entering a dark room where an armed *PERP* may be waiting. An officer going in can make a good target standing in the mouth of the *FATAL FUNNEL*, particularly if he or she is silhouetted. Here the flashlight roll can be used. It is best done with two officers flanking the doorway. One officer places the flashlight in the doorway, lens facing in, then turns it on and pushes it so it rolls across the doorway, beaming light inside. The other officer grasps the light and repeats the procedure if necessary.

flight deck

A hospital ward for drug users who have had mental breakdowns.

flimflam

Deceptive, illegal activities; a *CON*.

This phrase carries with it a sense of almost harmless chicanery, perhaps because the phrase itself is nonsensical; but the work of the flimflam artist can be quite devastating.

The origin of the term is likely onamatopeic and contemptuous, like fidfad, skimble-skamble, and whimwham.

See also *BUNCO*.

flip

When someone facing jail becomes an *INFORMANT* to reduce or eliminate a prison sentence; also called *roll over* and *turn*.

These days it seems that law enforcement agencies have become more aware of the value of getting one *BAD GUY* to turn against another. This is usually accomplished by offering the informant a lighter sentence—or no sentence at all—in return for testimony. In recent years, two of the more famous flips were Henry Hill and Sammy "The Bull" Gravano; both faced life in prison when they flipped. Their testimony resulted in long prison terms for high-ranking mafiosi.

Criminals have also learned the value of flipping, and more and more are doing it. The saying "There's no honor among thieves" is amply borne out.

flip-flop

In male prisons, to take turns assuming male and female (i.e., dominant and passive) roles in a sexual relationship.

flippers

Heterosexual females who assume a lesbian identity while in prison but return to heterosexuality when they leave.

floater

A *DECEASED* who has been floating in water.

A floater found in water is called a *wet floater;* one found out of water but exhibiting the same physical characteristics of one who has been in the water is a *dry floater.*

Police say that floaters are among the most noisome-looking corpses. A floater will be bloated, have "washer woman" (wrinkled) skin, be filled with gas, and have some skin missing or ready to come off. Wet floaters often have been nibbled on by marine life, and marine life is often found inside the body. Putrefecation generates gas, causing the body to bloat (see also *DEATH FART*).

Floater has been around since the turn of the century. In *How the Other Half Lives* (1891), author Jacob Riis said, "Floaters come ashore every now and then with pockets picked inside out, not always evidence of a post-mortem inspection by dock-rats."

flopped back

To be demoted from plainclothes to uniform duty.

An officer demoted to uniformed duty in New York is sometimes said to have been "flopped back to the bag." A demotion usually carries a transfer to *SIBERIA,* a precinct that is highly undesirable for one reason or another.

flute

A whiskey bottle secreted in a bag.

Both cops and criminals carry flutes to be surreptitiously sipped when needed.

According to *Oxford English Dictionary,* the origin of this term is likely a glass wine bottle that looked like a flute and was so dubbed.

See also *SHOOTER.*

following that cloud

Searching for drugs.

foot post

See *BEAT.*

foot search

Police search of an area by foot.

Some police departments may employ helicopters for searches, and all will occasionally use vehicles, but the foot search remains the most thorough.

Fort Apache

The 41st Precinct in New York City.

In the 1960s the Simpson Street station of the NYPD in the Bronx was infamous, a burned-out precinct filled with dilapidated buildings and an angry, hopeless populace that was besieged by criminals. Nicknamed Fort Apache, it became synonymous with the worst a police precinct could be.

Tom Walker explained the nickname in his book *Fort Apache.* Walker was the commanding officer there during its heyday. He says that there was once a dispute between police and citizens that so enraged the citizenry that they stormed the stationhouse. Walker detailed it in his Introduction:

"Several officers in the rear fire a volley over the heads of the crowd. In the confusion, Lotto and his men have time to retreat. The second volley forces the rest of the group back into the street. One of the mob's inciters, a Black named Oscar Brown and a friend of the arrested man, is cut down by a bat as he charges Lotto with a chain. By then, the field units have arrived and split the attackers into several containable groups. Sergeant Nat Clitter, the desk man who has called in a *TEN THIRTEEN,* has also called the Commissioner's office and was holding the phone in his hand waiting for someone to come on.

"Then he heard a tiny voice coming from the receiver: 'This is the Commissioner's Office. What the hell is going on?' Clitter looks at the receiver as if he could break it in two.

"'What the hell do you think is going on?' he screams. 'This is Fort Apache!' And he hangs up."

And the name—taken from a 1948 movie starring John Wayne—stuck.

forty

A 40-ounce bottle of malt liquor.

People who hang out on the *STREET* often carry beer and whiskey in paper bags because it's illegal to drink alcohol openly in public. Cops won't hassle them as long as the can or bottle is concealed in paper, even though it's obvious they're drinking. Colt Forty-Five is one of the more popular street drinks, probably because it has a high alcohol content. The bottle holds 40 ounces of liquid, hence the term.

fracture match

Method of determining whether a car was involved in an accident.

Accident investigators say that one of the best tools they have in establishing complicity in an accident is the fracture match—matching a piece of broken material left at the accident scene with the damaged vehicle suspected to have been involved. For example, someone may be hit by a car, but the driver flees, leaving behind only a small chunk of the bumper. For investigators this can be like finding gold. If they can find the damaged vehicle, all they have to do is fit the missing piece to it. They don't need much. Even a flake of paint that has chipped off can be matched.

Surprisingly, investigators say that cars that have been involved in an accident years before may still bear the scars of the encounter and a fracture match could be made.

See also *BUMPER FRACTURES* and *HIT-AND-RUN*.

frame

The calculated fabrication of evidence to make it seem as if an innocent party is guilty of a crime.

This is sometimes done to a particularly notorious criminal whom the police can't get any other way. Police may *PLANT* incriminating evidence but take care that all subsequent action is meticulously legal to ensure a conviction.

The origin of the word is unclear, and though frame has many different definitions, the abiding one is of assembling something, structuring it, building it. Hence, one builds a false case against someone else.

freebase

Cocaine purified by heating with ether; to smoke the fumes or the residue of the purified cocaine; the entire process of purifying the cocaine and smoking the residue.

This term exploded worldwide into the public consciousness when actor Richard Pryor almost lost his life freebasing. "A police lieutenant said that Mr. Pryor had told a doctor that the accident happened while he was trying to make 'freebase,' a cocaine derivative produced with the help of ether" (*New York Times,* June 13, 1980).

Two other terms for the process are *chase* and *ghost-busting.* Someone who freebases is called a *basehead.*

freeze

Police command that means "do not move."

Catching someone in the act of committing a crime is a high-stress, volatile situation that is fraught with peril for the police officer and the *PERP.* The officer needs terminology that will defuse the situation with clarity and force; the term freeze does this quite well.

fresh

Cool, up-to-date.

The term is not used as much as it used to be. More common today is the term *PHAT.*

front guy

Someone who represents another person in a criminal transaction.

fry

See *BURN*.

fuck slobs

Curse that the members of the Los Angeles gang *CRIPS* use to describe the *BLOODS,* their archenemies in the city.

funny money

Counterfeit money.

Counterfeiting is still quite common, and each year countless millions of counterfeit bills are put into circulation. Today's counterfeiters use much more sophisticated equipment for making funny money, or *queer,* than earlier counterfeiters.

The higher the denomination of the bill, the more scrutiny it gets, so if the counterfeiter is willing to create bills of lower denomination, chances of detection are reduced. One counterfeiter produced only $1 bills for 35 years, *DROPPING* (putting into circulation) an estimated $7 million before he was caught. Most commonly counterfeited is the $100 bill.

G

One thousand dollars' worth of drugs.

gag order

An order by a court to the participants in a trial not to publicly discuss the case.

Judges often impose gag orders on participants in a trial where talking about it could favor the prosecution or defense unfairly.

gang

A collection of criminals.

By 1400 it meant collections of things that went together, and in the early 1700s it had collected a negative meaning. Said Thomas Birch in *The Court and Times of Charles I:* "Nut the pirate . . . with all his gang of varlets."

gang banger

Gang member.

gangbuster

A law enforcement officer.

This term has been around quite awhile and is slightly archaic but still used fairly often.

gang sign

Hand signals used by gang members to identify each other.

Gang hand signals used by gang members identify not only the gang they're affiliated with but also the *SET,* or subdivision, of the gang they belong to.

garbage head

Someone who abuses drugs.

gat

A handgun.

The name derives from Gatling gun, a type of machine gun. The term gat has an archaic flavor, but it is still used, mostly with tongue in cheek but in some inner-city communities with grave seriousness.

See also *HARDWARE, HEAT, HEATER, PIECE,* and *TWENTY-TWO.*

gate

To be released from prison.

geek monster

Someone addicted to crack.

gentleman rapist

A rapist who thinks of himself as a gentleman despite his actions; also known as the *power assurance rapist.*

A gentleman rapist is characterized by Chicago police as someone who doesn't view the rape as an unwanted and violent assault. Although usually a sloppy man with poor sanitary habits, a gentleman rapist may dress up and apply some cologne before committing the rape. When he assaults his victim, he will use little or no physical force, except perhaps a slap or two, and he will talk with her, urging her to characterize him as a great lover.

He misinterprets her reactions. When leaving, he may smile to her and she will wanly smile back, and he will think she is saying thank you when all she is thinking is that she's glad he's leaving and glad to be alive.

get a gift

See *BUY.*

get down

1. In prison, inmates fighting.

   This appears to be a shortened version of "to get down on," which referred to a hostility of one group toward another. In *Quad's Odds* (1875) there is a line "The adult male population of the village got down on John Anderson Tompkins," but today it's gone beyond that—the circle of hostility in prisons is complete and inmates fight with one another.

2. Inject a drug.

   See also *FIX*.

get fast

To cheat one's criminal partner out of cash or goods.

This term apparently arose from the idea of "pulling a fast one" on someone.

get in someone's face

In prison, to intrude in someone's affairs.

get off

To not have to serve a prison sentence or to serve one that has been greatly reduced.

There are various reasons why someone gets off when tried in court: There can be a straight acquittal; the judge may hand down light sentences; or the prisoner's lawyer may *PLEA BARGAIN*.

get paid

In gangland, to get money for illegal activities.

One may get paid for a robbery, hijacking, or selling drugs. The key is that the money comes from a criminal offense.

get the button

To become a *MADE MAN* in the *MAFIA*.

See also *BUTTON MAN*.

get through

See *BUY*.

ghost-busting

See *FREEBASE*.

girl

See *QUEEN*.

girlfriend

A prostitute.

This term is used primarily by pimps.

git-go

In prison, the start or beginning of something.

glad rag

A rag soaked in gasoline or paint, then sniffed.

The phrase refers to the *HIGH* one gets when sniffing gasoline or paint. Many deaths have been associated with the practice, and young people in particular have suffered brain damage.

The use of glad rags is difficult to control because paint and gas are over-the-counter items. They're easy to buy—and use illegally— though some jurisdictions mandate that a person must be 18 or older to purchase spray paint.

go down

1. In prison, when something happens, usually unexpectedly.
2. To occur, to happen, usually in a dangerous sense.

   Many law enforcement officers use this term, particularly when referring to something that involves personal danger, such as a drug bust. For example, when officers are in position to make the raid, or *BUST,* and the commanding officer gives them the signal, some cop is sure to say "It's going down."

gold shield

A detective in the NYPD.

Few positions in police work generate more respect than a gold shield in the NYPD. It means that a cop has been selected from the ranks because of intelligence, wit, style, and nerve. It means that the cop is special.

In the past, detectives have also been known as *brains.*

golden shower

One person urinating on another for sexual stimulation.

Largely an activity of some homosexuals, golden showers are part of the *B & D* scene, in which people take pleasure in being dominated or defiled. Police view it, like other perverse sexual activities, to be of possible importance in some future investigation.

Golden showers are far more common than generally known, and a few homosexual groups sometimes have parties that are billed as that.

go native

When a police officer suffers a mental breakdown.

During the time a cop goes native, he or she drinks and/or takes drugs, carouses, and sometimes ignores personal hygiene. The condition signifies an emotional crisis and is usually temporary.

See also *BURNOUT.*

gone shot to the curb

Someone who has lost everything because of an addiction to *CRACK*.

good fella

See *WISE GUY.*

good go

When a buyer receives the right amount of drugs for the money paid.

good lick

Quality drugs.

good time

When a prisoner has one-third of his sentence cut because he has done his time adhering to the rules and regulations.

See also *SHORT-TIMER.*

goon

An enforcer for organized crime.

In the sixteenth century the term "gony" meant an oaf, or simpleton, and goon probably derived from that. Another theory has it arising from the Hindu term "gunda," a hired thug.

During the rise of the labor movement in America, it came to describe the musclebound bat-wielding types employed by companies seeking to remain union-free, but it gradually changed to mean a strong-arm type for the *MOB*. In his novel *All American*, Peter Maas portrays a typical goon as a neckless troglodyte whose only function in life seems to be whacking other people over the head with an iron pipe when bid to do so by his boss. "Gorilla" is another term synonymous with goon.

gopher

See *MULE*.

got it going on

Selling drugs rapidly.

goyakod

Acronym for "Get off your ass and knock on doors."

This is a term used by detectives to describe an aspect of *CANVASSING,* the questioning of potential witnesses of a crime. In New York City, one highly experienced homicide sergeant was heard to say that nothing beats goyakod in an investigation.

GP

See *HORSESHIT.*

grade money

System of pay escalation for detectives.

In New York, as a detective advances through the ranks, he or she gets increases in pay called grade money. There are three grades, and normally a person will work an entire career before achieving first-grade status.

graduate

1. Stop using drugs.
2. Go on to stronger drugs than used in the past.

grand jury

A jury assembled to determine if a case contains sufficient evidence to convict a person of a particular crime.

Grand juries have been around since the twelfth century, and during the American Revolution they were made a permanent part of American jurisprudence. The intention of the founding fathers was simple: to prevent prosecutors from indicting citizens for *FELONY* crimes without a jury deciding first whether there was *PROBABLE CAUSE* that the person had committed the crime.

Over time this original purpose has been somewhat diluted, and many people believe that grand juries, which are not set up like trials in terms of evidence and other significant procedures, have become tools for prosecutors to indict. In a landmark case in California in the 1980s, *Hurtado* v. *California,* the Supreme Court said that the grand jury was not necessary for due process of law under the Fourteenth Amendment. A number of states responded by abolishing grand juries.

Aside from being seen as a tool for prosecutors, grand juries are also viewed as being composed mainly of people who are not representative of the general population. In fact, most are composed of elderly white monied males and have been given the nickname *blue ribbon jury.* The composition of a grand jury will ultimately reflect which crimes are prosecuted and which are not.

grasseater

Police officer who takes small, insignificant bribes.

Down through the years, police officers have received small items free from merchants or restaurant owners—a "civil service discount"—either because it was expected, or because of the perception that it's always a good idea to have the police on your side.

The term grasseater describes such activities, which are technically bribes (favored treatment). The term "grasseating" came out during hearings by the Knapp Commission, which investigated corruption in the NYPD in the 1960s as part of the testimony of Sergeant William Phillips, himself a *MEATEATER,* a far more serious bribe taker.

Grasseater is no longer a common term.

See also *DIRTY.*

grays (in)

A trainee in the Police Academy.

Most police departments supply officers with gray uniforms while in training.

See also *ROOKIE*.

grave wax

Slang term for the waxy substance adipocere, which forms on bodies that are buried in moist places.

graveyard shifts

Night tours for the police, usually after midnight.

The term has been used by the general public since the early 1900s to describe any work done by anyone after midnight. In his 1966 novel *Doll*, Ed McBain defines the phrase: "The afternoon shift is from 4 P.M. to midnight. And the graveyard shift is midnight to 8 A.M."

grease

Money.

See also *GREEN STUFF, C-NOTE, HALF-A-LARGE, LARGE,* and *SCRATCH*.

green light

Authorization for police to assault a *HOSTAGE TAKER*.

In the Midwest, when all negotiation with a hostage taker fails and there is no more talk and no other option, police say assault is all that's left. They call this "getting the green light." The hostage taker may be fired on or gassed, but the action will be violent. The great majority of hostage/barricade situations are resolved before this point is reached—and everyone stays alive.

green stuff, greens, green goods

Cash money.

See also *C-NOTE, GREASE, HALF-A-LARGE, LARGE,* and *SCRATCH*.

grilled

When police intensely question a *SUSPECT* or *PERPETRATOR.*

Since the late 1800s standard English has defined the term as intense questioning. It seems natural that it would find its way into the lingo of law enforcement, because intense questioning of people is quite common. The term does have a slightly archaic feel to it, but police still use it frequently.

Common in the past—but still practiced in certain jurisdictions—was the beating of suspects. Police are quite adept at doing this without leaving any marks. One trick is to place a telephone book on the suspect, then whack the book with a pipe. The suspect can feel the blows, but the force is too dispersed to leave a mark. One PD used to beat the book with a pipe painted pink with yellow polka dots. If the suspects ever brought charges, they would hardly sound credible describing being beaten with a pipe that was pink with yellow polka dots.

ground ball

See *GROUNDER.*

ground control

A guide or caretaker during a hallucinogenic experience.
See also *BABY-SIT.*

grounder

An easy case to prosecute or solve; also known as a *ground ball.*

The term is used by both prosecutors and cops. For example, an assault has occurred, and the prosecutor has the weapon involved, fingerprints on the weapon, and three eyewitnesses. It will be easy to get a conviction. For homicide investigators, such cases also include family disputes gone bad or a fight that escalates into a homicide.

It's easy to see why family killings are simple to solve. Everyone knows each other, and there is usually a history of chaos before the homicide occurs. People around the family know who killed whom and why.

A fight that escalates into a homicide usually has witnesses. Police talk to the witnesses and an arrest is usually made fairly quickly.

Drug killings are also somewhat easy to solve. By talking to people on the street, police know the motive (so-and-so ripped so-and-so off) and the killer. Still, it might be difficult to get a conviction because witnesses are fearful of testifying against drug dealers.

Grounders are also known as *SLAM DUNKS*. The opposite of a grounder is a *MYSTERY,* also known as a *whodunit* or *puzzle.*

g'ster

A gangster.

Short for "gangster," this word is commonly used to describe gang members in black communities. Within the gang subculture, it is a complimentary term.

gump

In the Midwest, a male transvestite prostitute.

Male transvestites account for an astonishing percentage (over 50 percent) of the prostitutes on the street today, and many do such a good job of dressing like women that it's initially impossible to tell that they aren't.

In these days of AIDS, unprotected sex with any prostitute is dangerous, but it's doubly hazardous with gumps. Many are HIV-positive or have full-blown AIDS. The term originally meant chicken. Eric Partridge quotes Jack Black in *You Can't Win* (1926): "I've got a gump in my bindle. . . . He unrolled his blankets and produced a chicken, big and fat." Though there is no clear connection, it may be related to *CHICKENS,* young boys who are preyed upon by some male homosexuals called *CHICKEN HAWKS.*

See also *CALL GIRL, GIRLFRIEND, STREET GIRL,* and *STREET-WALKER.*

gun run

When police respond to a situation where it is known that the *PERPS* have guns.

A gun run is one of the most feared things police face because they know their lives are in imminent danger. "Particularly," said one cop, "because of the way the bad guys are armed today. They have TEC 9s and Uzis and we have handguns and shotguns."

gutter junkie

Addict who relies on others to obtain drugs.

H

half-a-large

Five hundred dollars.

See also *GREEN STUFF, LARGE.*

half-load

Fifteen *DECKS* of heroin.

This is a unit of sale of heroin.

half-piece

One half-ounce of heroin or cocaine.

hardware

A gun or guns.

See also *GAT, HEAT,* and *HEATER.*

hash

Short for hashish, the resinous secretions of the cannabis (marijuana) plant.

The Middle East is the main source for this drug. It was made famous by the motion picture *Midnight Express,* which portrayed American Billy Hayes's ordeal of being caught trying to board a plane in Turkey with a load of hash and subsequently confined to a brutal Turkish prison.

To prepare hash, the resinous secretions are collected, dried, and then compressed into a variety of forms, including balls and *soles,* which is one street name for the drug because they look like the soles of shoes.

hash, black

Opium mixed with hashish.

have a hardon for

In prison, to have a bad feeling toward someone.

If one inmate has a "hardon" for another, it usually ends in violence.

have heart

To have courage.

This term is used by prison inmates.

hawala, or hundi

South Asian nonbanking financial systems used for centuries to move money, gold, and consumer goods across the subcontinent to Europe and the Middle East.

This network is often used by drug smugglers.

See also *MONEY LAUNDERING*.

head up

In gang terminology, to fight with someone.

hearsay evidence

Evidence based on what one person heard another say.

Whether written or oral, hearsay evidence is not considered very strong evidence.

heat

1. To put pressure on a criminal or criminal organization through arrests, raids, and other forms of harassment.

   Law enforcement groups "put the heat on" criminals for a number of reasons. For example, pressure is always beefed up when a police officer has been killed. In the game of cops versus robbers, one of the rules is that if a member of a criminal organization kills a cop, the whole gang can expect all kinds of pressure, including arrests, raids, and just being rousted until the killer is arrested.

   A few years back when a *DEA* officer was shot to death by a small-time hood named Gus Stabile, the pressure on *THE MOB* to which he was affiliated became unbearable. It was suggested that Gus was in a precarious position, that it was a question of who would get him first. The mob did—Gus was found shot to death in a car.

Law enforcement can feel the heat too. When particularly nasty and highly publicized crimes are committed (such as in the "Son of Sam" case), the efforts of law enforcement groups are put under a microscope, examined daily in the newspapers and on TV, and evaluated by millions.

The term has been around since the 1920s. "The greatest difficulty for such a mob was to avoid another's heat. It's not so much your own heat you got to watch, but you're apt to run into a bunch of hoosiers out looking for another outfit just hot from some caper" (*American Mercury,* May 1928).

2. A gun.

See also *GAT, HEATER, PIECE,* and *TWENTY-TWO.*

heater

Gun.

This term goes back to the 1920s. "Aw, put up your heaters. If you *BUMP* me you don't git anywheres" (*Detective Fiction Weekly,* November 9, 1928). It is still used, even though the user will probably be aware that the term is slightly archaic.

See also *GAT, HEAT, PIECE,* and *TWENTY-TWO.*

heeled

Having plenty of money.

heist

Armed robbery.

This is the most familiar term used by police to describe a crime that involves a perpetrator with a weapon, usually a gun.

Years ago, the term was used for other types of robbery, such as burglary, but now it only applies to armed robbery.

hello phones

Telephone lines that mob informers use to reach their FBI contacts.

Such phones are specially located in FBI offices, and the people who answer them say "Hello," rather than identifying their affiliation.

Henry Lee Lucas Memorial Highway

The stretch of I-75 that runs from I-10 south to Gainesville, Florida.

In the 1970s Henry Lee Lucas, one of the most infamous murderers of the century—a man who may have killed more than 300 people—traveled the stretch of I-10 that began near Laredo, Texas, and ended at the I-75 exit to Gainesville, apparently hitchhiking or picking up hitchhikers, murdering them, and then dumping their bodies along that short stretch of I-75. When Lucas confessed, it gave rise to the name.

heroin

See *HORSE.*

hesitation marks

Cuts on the wrists or neck of a suicide victim that indicate that the person who committed suicide hesitated before making the fatal cut(s).

Such marks do not always reflect suicide. As Vernon Geberth points out in *Practical Homicide Investigation,* "an assailant who is knowledgeable about these (marks) might leave similar markings to cover up a homicide."

high

To be under the influence of drugs.

Most illegal drugs produce a peaceful, happy, content feeling in the user, and high is probably the most common term used to describe the experience. Other terms for being under the influence of drugs include the following:

all lit up	lit up
blasted	loaded
charged up	on a trip
coasting	riding the wave
cranked up	shot down
flying	stoned
hopped up	strung out

hit

1. A murder by contract.

    This is the most common name used for a *MOB* murder; it is also used frequently by law enforcement personnel. The threat of death is the ultimate weapon used by organized crime to control people. The rule is simple: Do it my way or be killed.

    For years, if you were going to be hit by the *MAFIA,* you could expect that a certain decorum would be observed: They wouldn't *DO* you in front of your family. That has changed. The most dramatic example was the killing of Joey "Crazy Joe" Gallo, a renegade mafioso who was shot by two gunmen while dining with his wife in Umberto's Clam House in New York City.

    The time to worry about being hit is when you are aware of having committed a fatal offense (such as stealing drugs) and are subsequently invited somewhere by a close friend. This is frequently the way a hit is achieved: The friend has been forced to set you up.

    Today the various gangs are much more violent than in the past. Indeed, the level of violence is mind boggling, and perhaps most shocking are the Colombians. They not only don't care about your family observing you being killed, but will hit the entire family because of your transgressions.

    Hit first showed up in print in America in 1971 in *Sleep is for the Rich* by D. McKenzie: "I got scared and called the whole thing off. Someone else must have made the hit."

    See also *HIT MAN.*

2. To take a drug.

    Ed McBain used the term in his 1964 novel, *Like Love:* "A narcotics cop will insist on examining a prostitute's thighs for hit marks, even when he knows she couldn't possibly be a junkie."

    See also *FIX.*

3. Obtain a drug.

    Addicts, particularly those who are "strung out," will go to extraordinary lengths to obtain drugs, up to and including selling their bodies, committing burglaries, and worse. One female inmate in Riker's Island indicated this when she said that while on the street, she would do "anything for my addiction," more

113

than she would do even for her newborn baby. The term was first used in print in the May 1951 issue of the *National Education Journal:* "They are anxious to make a 'connection,' 'score,' or 'hit'."

See also *BUY* and *SCORE*.

4. Screening a suspect's background for a criminal record and discovering there is an outstanding violation. *The Trooper,* a New York State Police magazine, reported an incident in which a man had been stopped for speeding, and upon investigation by officers it was determined that the man did not have a driver's license. Searching the car, "several pieces of identification were found, all with the same date of birth, but with different names. By using different combinations of names, a File 12 'hit' from the New York City Police Department was obtained . . . and it was learned that the man was wanted for murder."

See also *PRIORS* and *YELLOW SHEET.*

hit-and-run

An automobile accident in which the responsible driver illegally flees the scene.

First use of the phrase was recorded in 1924 by *Scientific American,* in an article that envisioned eliminating hit-and-run accidents if the bumper could somehow be mechanically linked to the vehicle's ability to move—or not move. "With the bumper in circuit with the ignition, there would be no more 'hit and run' driving." The idea, it seems, was that if the car couldn't go forward after hitting a person or another vehicle, no one could really run away.

While most people think of a hit-and-run as a very serious crime, it is not viewed so by the law. In fact, it is only a Class 1 misdemeanor, which carries a penalty of up to a year in prison. The only way a serious penalty can be meted out is to upgrade the crime to "reckless homicide." That is, if you are driving recklessly in an area—say, a crowded street—where it's clear that you shouldn't, you can receive up to five years.

Accident investigators say that they approach all fatal accidents as murders. "You'd be surprised," said one cop, "on how many people are killed deliberately. These days we find that a lot of drug dealers take each other out this way."

One of the worst things about a hit-and-run accident is that more than occasionally the victim could have survived if only the hit-and-run driver had not fled and left the person to die without medical assistance.

See also *BUMPER FRACTURE* and *FRACTURE MATCH*.

hit man

Person who carries out a contract killing.

A hit man may be a professional killer, also known as a *MECHANIC,* or someone new to an organized crime group who has to prove his loyalty and mettle by murdering someone.

The preferred weapon for hit men is the twenty-two pistol. While not a powerful gun, it does the job very well.

hold

To possess drugs.

holding tank

A cell within a prison where new inmates are held until they are assigned permanent cells; also called a *BULL PEN*.

hold your integrity

In the California area, an exhortation by a commanding officer to other officers to hold their positions as they advance into a disruptive situation, such as a civil riot.

Just how difficult it can be to hold one's integrity was wonderfully expressed by Joseph Wambaugh in *The New Centurions* when he described a trio of cops driving toward the riot-riddled Watts area of Los Angeles, the horizon aflame, in the 1960s. Two veteran cops were sitting in the front seat of the vehicle, a rookie was in the back. For a long time the rookie was silent, so one of the cops in front finally turned to ask him how he was doing. "I want," he said simply, "my teddy."

hole

See *BLACK HOLE*.

homicidal triangle

The three kinds of aggressive behavior exhibited by *SERIAL MURDERERS* in childhood that are predictive of sociopathic behavior and homicide: enuresis (bedwetting), cruelty to animals, and fire-setting.

Some psychologists say that when a child exhibits all these behavioral characteristics, he (they occur mostly in males) is far more likely to eventually commit homicide than someone without these characteristics. Even if just two of the characteristics are present, it is a dangerous sign.

The backgrounds of a number of serial murderers show extreme cruelty to animals, as well as pyromania. For example, Henry Lee Lucas, perhaps the worst serial murderer of all, skinned small animals alive when he was ten. Robert Hanson, who killed prostitutes in Alaska, set many fires as a youth in Pocahontas, Iowa. Edmund Kemper, who killed six coeds in northern California, was also very cruel to animals.

The first observers of this triad were D. S. Hellman and N. Blackman in "Enuresis, Firesetting, and Cruelty to Animals: A Triad Predictive of Adult Crime," which appeared in the June 1966 issue of the *American Journal of Psychiatry*. Many law enforcement personnel feel that the three behavioral activities are very accurate predictors.

honeymoon

Early stages of drug use, before addiction develops.

hood

Short for hoodlum, a criminal or disreputable person.

There are many theories about the origin of the word. Some say that it refers to a leader of hooded thugs in San Francisco; others say that it derives from the Bavarian word *hydelum*.

Its first appearance in print may have been in San Francisco on April 27, 1871, when a news item in the *Daily Union* reported that two " 'hoodlums' [the quotations are theirs, possibly indicating unfamiliarity with the word] who were arrested in the Sarsfield guard picnic excursion on Sunday last, are doing duty in the chain gang on the streets of that city, which, together with the fact that a third 'hoodlum' got his throat cut by an Indian at the same place, gives great satisfaction to our citizens."

The only certainty is that the term is used a lot. In fact, if you ask a cop for a brief description of a criminal's occupation, you'll probably hear something like "He's a hood."

'hood

Short for neighborhood, this term is used by blacks.

Used to describe a predominantly black neighborhood, it has been known for years within black communities and by younger people of all ethnic origins. But it probably did not enter the public consciousness until the motion picture *Boyz N the Hood* came out in 1991. The film was nominated for a number of Academy Awards, and the term was widely publicized.

hook

1. A tow truck.

   The main feature of a tow truck, of course, is the hook on the back, which is secured to a car and then the car is lifted, making its journey on only one pair of tires. Police commonly use hooks to tow away illegally parked cars.

2. Someone a police officer knows who can get the officer favored treatment.

   See also *ANGEL*.

hooked

Addicted to a drug.

The origin of the term is unclear, but it may well have to do with the concept of being on a hook like a fish, unable to get off.

homeboy

Someone who is wise to the streets, "one of the boys."

Homeboy is a very common term today. Gang members as well as others use it; it implies know-how and *HEART*. While primarily used in the black community, the term is also used by non-blacks.

Its origins are obscure, but it may refer to boys who were sent to homes (places of detention, juvenile correctional facilities). One reference in the *Oxford English Dictionary* says that it refers to a boy brought up in an orphanage or institution, but another—and a more likely one—says, "Homeboy is a slang expression particularly in vogue among students at Southern Negro colleges. . . . Home boy and similar forms, such as home girl and home people, denote individuals who come from the same home town as the speaker."

horn

To inhale a drug.

horse

Common slang for heroin.

Heroin got its start in Germany around the turn of the century, when it was synthesized from morphine by the Bayer Company. For quite a while it was manufactured and distributed without anyone being aware of its addictive qualities, but by 1914 the Harrison Narcotics Act signaled comprehensive control of it.

Heroin comes in many forms. In its pure state it is white and has a bitter taste. Colored heroin—white to dark brown and shades in between—occurs because dealers add substances such as food coloring, cocoa, or brown sugar.

Pure heroin is rarely sold on the street. A single *BAG* of heroin—the basic term for a saleable unit—contains about 100 milligrams of material with 5 percent of it heroin. To increase the bulk sold on the street, additives are mixed with the heroin in ratios from 9:1 to 99:1.

The origin of the term is not clear, but it was first in print in *Time* magazine, August 28, 1950: "There are the usual thrill seekers who take goof balls . . . quite often ending up as confirmed addicts of . . . heroin (H, horse, white stuff)."

Many other terms are used for heroin, including:

AIP (from Afghanistan, Iran, and Pakistan)
antifreeze
atom bomb (heroin mixed with marijuana)
Aunt Hazel
bad seed
ballot
beast
Belushi (heroin and cocaine)
big bag
big H
big Harry
bindle
birdie powder
black pearl
black stuff
black tar

blanco
bomb
bombido
bombita
bonita
boy
bozo
brick gum
brown
brown rhine
brown sugar
bundle
butu
caballo
caca
capital H
caps
carga
carne
Charley
chasing the dragon (heroin and
  crack)
chieva
Chinese red
chip
climax
cotics
courage pills
cura
deuce
dirt
dog food
dogie
dooley
dope
dreck
duji

dust
dynamite (heroin mixed with
  cocaine)
dyno
dyno-pure
el diablito (heroin, marijuana,
  cocaine, and PCP)
el diablo (heroin, marijuana,
  and cocaine)
eight-ball (heroin mixed with
  crack)
eight
estuffa
ferry dust
flamethrowers (heroin, cocaine,
  and tobacco)
foo-foo stuff
foolish powder
galloping horse
gamot
gato
George smack
girl
glacines
golden girl
golpe
good H
goofball (heroin and cocaine)
HRN
hache
hairy
hard candy
hard stuff
Harry
Hazel
H caps
heaven dust

Helen
hell dust
Henry
hero
heroina
herone
hero of the underworld
hessle
him
hombre
horning
isda
jee-gee
jive
jive doo-jee
jojee
Jones
joy powder
joy flakes
junk
kabayo
LBJ
lemonade
little bomb
matsakow
mayo
Mexican brown
Mexican horse
Mexican maid
Mexican mud
mojo
moonrock (heroin and crack)
morotgara
muzzle
new jack swing (heroin and
    morphine)
nickle bag
nikkle deck
nose
noise
number 8
ogoy
oil
old Steve
P-funk
pack
pangondalot
parachute
peg
perfect high
poison
polvo
poppy
powder
primo (heroin, cocaine, and
    tobacco)
pullborn
pure
racehorse Charlie
ragweed
Rambo
rane
red chicken
red eagle
red rock
reindeer dust
rhine
sack
salt
scag
scat
scate
Scott
shmeck/schmeck

skid

sleeper

slim

smoke (heroin and crack)

snow

snowball (heroin and cocaine)

speedball (heroin mixed with
  cocaine)

spider blue

stuff

sugar

sweet Jesus

sweet stuff

TNT

tar

taste

tecate

thing

tootsie roll

white boy

white girl

white junk

white lady

white nurse

white stuff

whiz bang (heroin and cocaine)

wings (heroin and cocaine)

wings

witch

witch hazel

horseshit

Prison-issue tobacco

Also called *GP,* for general population cigarettes.

hose job

Fellatio.

hostage taker

Anyone who takes hostages.

Police say that hostage takers are usually men, and the motive in 90 percent of the cases is women. There is commonly a disruption of some sort; the woman leaves the man; he goes berserk, gets a weapon, takes a hostage(s)—who could well be a member of his own family—and barricades himself against the world, ready to die and to kill the hostages.

Other hostage takers are criminals whose crimes go bad. They may have entered a premise for a holdup, and then someone pressed a silent alarm, and suddenly the street outside is swarming with police. The perpetrator grabs someone and gets into a standoff. Police say that such a situation usually turns out all right, because the hostage taker comes to realize that (1) the police are not going to go away and (2) he could be killed. Once he starts thinking about survival, he will surrender.

Other hostage takers are simply mentally ill or paranoid, and they have taken hostages because of real or imagined difficulties. Cops say that it's best to just listen to these people until they talk themselves out, and the police will hopefully be able to give them an alternative that they can take.

The most dangerous hostage takers are religious fanatics. As one Chicago cop in Connie Fletcher's *Pure Cop* put it, "He's listening to messages from God. How do you compete with God? Why would a religious fanatic even consider that you help him?"

In New York City a hostage taker is known as a *barricaded EDP* (emotionally disturbed person).

See also *DOUBLE WHAMMY, FATHER MULCAHY SYNDROME,* and *GREEN LIGHT.*

hot

Stolen.

The sense is that because the item is stolen it's too hot to handle and has to be disposed of quickly.

hot chair

In prison group therapy, the person who is being focused on by the rest of the group at a particular time; also called *hot seat.*

Such sessions are a regular part of many prison programs, because they help prisoners to vent feelings that otherwise might be bottled up and be released in some less appropriate way.

hot heroin

See *HOT SHOT.*

hot rod

To mechanically modify a gun, usually done by a police officer.

These modifications can take many forms, all designed to produce a better gun. Sometimes the officer will add a trigger shoe, which makes a trigger wider so it is easier to pull; other officers will modify safety features or remove screws. The end result of these modifications is often very bad.

A gun is composed of ten to twenty working parts, all designed to work together with balance and precision; modifying one or the other can affect this precision and make the gun more difficult to use or cause it to fail. "Unless a guy is a licensed gunsmith," says one gunshop owner, "hot rodding is an invitation to disaster."

hot seat

The electric chair.

On TV and in the movies, dying—or being killed—by electric chair is sanitized, the sharp edges of the reality blunted. The phrase hot seat first appeared in print in *The Saturday Evening Post* (of all places) on August 18, 1925: "A judge sentenced a boy fifteen years old to the electric chair . . . a newspaper reporter heard the lad say that he was not afraid to die in the 'hot seat.' " A variation on the phrase appeared in the January 1927 issue of *Flynns Weekly:* "I never shot nobody . . . Lotsa times I don't carry a gun. That's one thing I try to dodge—the hot chair." Another variation appeared in the book *Showgirl* by J. P. McEvoy in 1928: "I ought to get something for that don't you think? The chair maybe—better known as the hot squat."

hot shot

A fatal injection of a drug, usually heroin.

The term today means death from an excess of drugs, but when first used by William Burroughs it meant something entirely different, and more diabolical. "Poison," he said in *Junkie* (1972), "usually strychnine, passed to an addict as junk. The peddler sometimes slips a hot shot to an addict who is giving information to the law." *Hot Heroin* is another name for this.

E. E. Landy in *Underground Dictionary* (1972) adds, "Injection of a drug that is a higher potency than the addict is used to." Another common name for causing death by an excessive intake of drugs is *OD* (overdose).

hot squat

See *HOT SEAT.*

house

A prison cell.

Prisoners regard their cells as their houses or homes.

See also *CELL* and *REAL ESTATE*.

hui kuan

Chinese family-oriented underground banking system used by
MONEY LAUNDERERS.

hyoid bone

Small U-shaped bone at the base of the tongue.

Homicide investigators are very familiar with the hyoid bone,
which is frequently broken during manual strangulation.

I

IAD

Internal affairs division.

The cops in this division investigate wrongdoing by other cops. They are widely hated in police departments because they are viewed as traitors, informants on their brother officers. It does not matter that what they do has a good purpose; it matters only that they are informing on other police officers.

It takes, as one might guess, a special kind of individual to do such work. Besides a thick skin, he or she must be willing to go against that sense of police brotherhood—the *BLUE WALL*—and to be treated like an outcast all the time.

Other officers say that many IAD investigators are idealists and very religious, that they see the world sharply in terms of good and evil, black and white. There are occasional shake-ups in IAD units, but rarely because of corruption.

See also *DIRTY* and *SHOOFLIES*.

ice

1. Jewelry.
2. To murder.

This was a very popular term in the 1960s, but as time went by the idea faded (or melted). Today it is only occasionally used and mostly by cops who came of age in the 1960s.

The term originated in black communities and gradually spread beyond. It refers to what happens physically when someone dies: The body cools, a process known as *ALGOR MORTIS*.

ID

1. Standard police term for a form of identification; for example, "Did he have any *ID* on him?"
2. To identify someone: "Could anyone ID the suspect?"

illegals

Anyone who comes into the United States illegally.

in

Connected with drug suppliers.

in flight

Someone who is under the influence of drugs.

High is a commonly used word for the experience of being on drugs; so when in flight, one is up high, soaring in the air.

informant

Someone who tells law enforcement authorities about the criminal activities of others.

In the movies and on television, investigators are often shown solving crimes by sheer Sherlock-Holmesian investigative acumen, but the reality is that over 90 percent of all crimes are solved based on intelligence supplied by informants. Most detectives use them regularly, and informants don't work free. Sometimes the pay is favored treatment, sometimes it's money, and sometimes, if the informant is an addict (and many are), the payment can be drugs. In the cop's mind, paying in drugs can be the lesser of two evils: To take down a big drug dealer, a few bags of heroin—or more—is insignificant. It is, however, a *FELONY*. But as one cop said, "I have committed many felonies in the pursuit of justice."

Criminals loathe informants; and once found out, an informant's life expectancy, particularly in prison, is short unless he or she goes into protective custody.

See also *FINK* and *FLIP.*

insider trading

Illegal exchange of information about a pending corporate takeover.

Although illegal under Securities and Exchange Commission rules, insider trading has been around for a long time. It seemed to be a crime of the 1980s only because in that decade it was done on a massive scale, with people like Ivan Boesky and Dennis Levine reaping millions upon millions of dollars, and the star of it all, Michael Milken, becoming a billionaire.

Insider trading works simply: One individual in the know tells another of the intent of one company to take over another. The insider can then buy and manipulate stock to reap maximum benefit from it. It is *WHITE COLLAR CRIME* at its most profitable.

intent

A legal concept that indicates that a perpetrator had the intention of committing a crime; that the crime was a clear and willful act.

invent

see *RACK.*

ivory tower (the)

In New York City, One Police Plaza, police headquarters.

This is, of course, a pejorative term that arose from the average cop's perception that the bosses don't understand what life is like on the *STREET,* even though many of them spent time there. "After a while," says one cop, "they forget what it was like."

In reality, the building is a reddish brown color and located well downtown in the city, contiguous to courts.

J

jack

1. To commit armed robbery.

   This term is used by gangs in the Los Angeles area.

2. Heroin in tablet form.

   This term was first defined by M. M. Glatt in *Drug Scene*.

jacked up

1. In prison, to be annoyed by guards over piddling matters; also known as having your buttons pushed.

   A lot of this sort harassment goes on in prison. Said one inmate about the Maryland State Prison, whose nickname is the House of Frankenstein, "It's not the time you do that's the hard thing, it's them dudes you got to do it with. Unless you watch your ass, someone will be trying to steal it, or kick it, or stuff it."

   Hence the pressure is great, and minor lapses in behavior may result in someone taking offense—with homicide the result.

2. To be under the influence of heroin.

jacket

An inmate's actual file, or his reputation.

Jacket comes from the idea of wearing something: One wears one's reputation like an article of clothing.

See *SNITCH JACKET*.

jailhouse lawyer

An inmate who is versed in criminal law and, though usually not an attorney, does all kinds of legal work for other inmates.

Many prisons have extensive law libraries; some states have even passed laws requiring that they have them. The lawsuits filed by jailhouse lawyers seldom meet with success, but in quite a few instances, inmates were released, because either the cases against them were unjust or the jailhouse mouthpiece was able to find a legal point that could result in a reversal.

jailhouse turnout

An inmate whose sexual preference changes in prison from heterosexual to homosexual.

This poses a very real problem for inmates who are young, good-looking, and relatively frail. There are always sexual predators on the loose looking for someone to "turn." To counteract this, some young prisoners start to "pump iron," or lift weights. Someone who is physically strong has less chance of getting raped or turned.

See also *JOCKER* and *MAYTAG*.

jack off the spike

To draw blood completely into a hypodermic needle to wash or rinse out any residue of the drug.

"Jack off" is sexual slang for masturbate. Drawing from that image, the hypodermic needle serves as the penis.

jakes

A regional term for uniformed police officers.

jam up

When one inmate puts another in a difficult situation.

For example, one prisoner might repeat a bigoted remark made by one convict about another. This is not the type of remark that is allowed to pass in prison. Retribution is called for; tolerating it signals weakness to other prisoners.

Also referred to as *put in a cross.*

Jane Doe

See *JOHN DOE.*

Jane Wayne syndrome

See *JOHN WAYNE SYNDROME.*

JD

Abbreviation for juvenile delinquent.

Jefferson Airplane

Paper match cut lengthwise in half to hold a partially smoked marijuana *JOINT.*

Term is derived from the rock group of the same name.

See also *ROACH* and *POT.*

jet

To run fast, usually away from law enforcement authorities.

Jewish lightning

Arson.

This New York area term comes from the idea that the fire is started in order to turn a profit on a business that is perhaps on its last legs. When arson is suspected—and arson investigators say that perhaps 15 percent of all fires are criminally set—the first suspect is usually the owner of the business. It is not difficult for the police to determine if a business is in trouble, but arson is a difficult crime to prove. But police are determined, and even after years they can knock on the door, proof in hand, and make an arrest.

The origin of Jewish lightning is unclear, but it most likely arose during the 1930s or 1940s, when bias against Jews was strong and vocal, particularly related to money.

See also *MEXICAN LIGHTNING* and *TORCH.*

jimmy

A tool, such as a flat crowbar, used to pry open a safe or a door, for example.

Though slightly archaic, the term is still used. The etymology is unclear, but in the mid-1850s the term jimmy was first used in this sense; it was a variant of "jemmy," a tool commonly used by burglars.

See also *SLIM JIM.*

jocker

A male prison inmate who is the protector in a homosexual relationship.

Young prisoners who want to protect themselves from unwanted attention sometimes form relationships with jockers, strong inmates who will protect them as long as they are faithful.

The term apparently comes from the sexual slang term "jock," which describes the genitals of a man or woman and which referred to a man living off the earnings of a prostitute in the late eighteenth century. The aspect of one person using another in return for protection was presumably retained in a meaning of the word that emerged in 1893, "a tramp who begs for him or acts as his catamite."

In *Blue Knight* (1976), Joseph Wambaugh referred to jockers: "Roxie hustles the guys who want a queen, and the kid goes after the ones who want a jocker. This jocker would probably become a queen himself."

See also *BACKER, JAILHOUSE TURNOUT,* and *MAYTAG.*

john

The client of a prostitute.

In the mid-1940s, prostitutes described clients by using the slang term for toilet and condom, both of which at one time were called a "Johnnie." Either term is contemptuous.

John Doe

An unidentified body.

It is sometimes impossible to identify corpses. The body may be in a state of advanced decomposition, unrecognizable and without fingerprints. Many people, such as indigents, runaways, and prostitutes, have no roots in a community. A person's fingerprints may not be on file with the FBI. When a corpse cannot be identified, it is classified as a John Doe or Jane Doe, and may eventually end up being buried in a potter's field (a public burial ground).

John Wayne syndrome

A feeling of invincibility in male police officers; the female counterpart is called a *JANE WAYNE SYNDROME.* Also known as the *Superman syndrome.*

This type of behavior is not beloved by other cops, because feeling you're immortal can lead to taking unnecessary risks that may result in your partner getting injured or killed.

Eventually, someone with this problem will be approached by other officers and told to either stop or be ostracized (put in a position where they may not get the support of other officers when needed).

The syndrome is named after the famous actor whose persona, more or less in all his pictures, was of a big, tough guy who would not take anything from anybody and would always win in the end. John Wayne portrayed an invulnerable hero—something that a real-life police officer is not.

joint

1. Prison.

    The origin of the word is unclear, but today it is fairly commonly used by people on both sides of the law to describe jail, particularly penitentiaries where long-term sentences are served. William Burroughs used the word in *Junkie* in 1953: "He said even the best thieves spend most of their time in the joint."

2. A marijuana cigarette.

    The origin of the term is not clear, but there are two possibilities, neither completely convincing.

    One is that it arose out of the idea of the joint as the "stem of a plant" as *Oxford English Dictionary* says, "from which a leaf or branch grows up (especially when thickened, as in grasses) so as to resemble a knee- or elbow-joint; a node." The connection here would be purely botanical: Marijuana is a plant; indeed, one of the many slang terms used to describe it is grass.

    The other possible origin connects it to an opium den. Years ago the word joint meant a place or house the Chinese ran for opium smokers. There might be some connection in terms of the *HIGH* received; opium gives a high, and so does marijuana.

    Other terms for a marijuana cigarette include jive stick, joy stick, nail, number, pack of rocks, panatella (large cigarette), pocket rocket, prescription, stick, straw, and Zol.

joy popping

see *CHIP*.

juggle
To sell drugs to support one's own habit.

juice
1. A corrupting influence; power.

    Police officers think of juice two ways: (1) money that can be used to influence events, or (2) power in general.
2. To lend money at usurious rates.

    "At least two murders and perhaps more have been connected to the *LOAN SHARK,* or 'juice' racket, as it is called here, as well as beatings and threats" (*New York Times,* June 9, 1968).

    See also *VIG.*

jumper
Someone who threatens, attempts, or succeeds in committing suicide by jumping.

Suicide by jumping is relatively rare in large cities, and it is almost unheard of in small towns because the buildings aren't tall enough. One police officer reported that he had patrolled the city for twenty-seven years both on foot and in a radio car and had never personally experienced a single jumper during that time. "Then one day," he said, "I experienced two—on the same day. One in the morning, one in the afternoon." So much for odds.

See also *DRY DIVE.*

junk
Illegal narcotics, particularly heroin.

Junk has been used to describe anything without value, ready to be discarded. In the sense of putting garbage in your veins, drugs as junk seems to be well understood. Since the 1920s and probably earlier, junk has been used to describe drugs in general and heroin in particular.

junkies
Drug addicts, usually heroin addicts.

This is undoubtedly the most common term used to describe heroin addicts and drug addicts in general.

K

keeper

An arrest that results in someone being held to face arraignment in court.

See also *BUST, COLLAR, FALL,* and *PINCH.*

keister stash

Illegal objects secreted in the rectum; also called a *keister stow.*

It is quite common for prisoners to secrete drugs and other illegal items in the rectum. When they are subjected to a *SKIN SEARCH* by prison personnel, they are required to spread their cheeks to see if something is hidden there.

See also *FINGER WAVE.*

key

One kilo metric weight (2.2 pounds) of an illegal drug.

kick

Get off a drug habit.

kickback place

In Los Angeles, a place where gang members relax.

kiddie dope

Prescription drugs.

killer

Murderer.

Many police still like to use the term killer instead of murderer because the word seems to sum up just what the person is.

Interestingly, no matter how often the word is used, it has a chilling edge.

kite

1. Form prisoners use to request an interview with a prison official.
2. A check drawn on insufficient funds or on a nonexistent account; a forged check.
3. A communication, particularly an illicit one, that a prisoner either smuggles out of prison or receives from someone outside prison.

    "Sometimes . . . prisoners manage to plant notes in various parts of the prison which are to be picked up by the intended recipient. This practice of 'shooting' contraband notes is known among prisoners as 'flying a kite' " (J. F. Fishman, *Crucibles of Crime*).

knock

See *BUST.*

lady

See *QUEEN*.

lajaras

In New York, Hispanic slang for a policeman.

It is a takeoff on O'Hara, an Irish name and, to many immigrant New Yorkers, a typical cop name because for years most NYPD members were Irish.

landline

Telephone.

In police departments, the two main ways to communicate are by radio and by telephone. In the days before cellular phones, communication by telephone meant that the electronic signals traveled along wires that were landed.

large (a)

One thousand dollars.

See also *GREASE, GREEN STUFF, HALF-A-LARGE, LETTUCE,* and *SCRATCH.*

latents

See *FINGERPRINTS*.

leads

Pieces of information that lead police in certain directions during the investigation of a crime.

Leads may come from many sources, including *PHYSICAL EVIDENCE* and oral tips, but all such clues point the investigator in a promising direction.

Popularized in TV, movies, and books, the terms that investigators exchange are familiar to most people: "Any leads?" "No, no leads at all."

lemonade
See *BLANKS*.

lettuce
Money.

See also *GREEN STUFF*.

lie detector
A machine used to detect physiological evidence of the tension that accompanies lying.

It measures blood pressure, heart rate, and respiration. A series of ordinary questions are posed, and measurements noted to establish what might be called the parameters of one's truthfulness; in other words, the physiological reactions of someone based on ordinary, truthful answers. Then questions relating to the crime are asked, and the physiological reactions are observed to see if they stay within truthful parameters.

Not everyone believes in the validity of lie detectors, but many law enforcement agencies do. The machine does presuppose a conscience: A person who is not being truthful will know it and have an adverse reaction if telling a lie. How a true sociopath—who feels no guilt—would react is moot.

lineup
A group of people viewed by a witness to a crime to try to identify the guilty party.

There are two types of lineups: one in which suspects are physically present; the other in which only photos of suspects are viewed by witnesses.

Lipton tea
See *BLANKS*.

lividity
Short for post mortem lividity, or *livor mortis,* the settling of the blood in the bottom portions of the body following death.

Lividity is an asset to investigators because it can tell them the approximate time of death and whether or not the body was moved.

Lividity occurs because the heart has stopped pumping blood to the various parts of the body. Since the blood's not moving, gravity causes it to settle. This usually starts within thirty minutes of death, and the process is complete within eight to ten hours of death.

Lividity can help investigators determine the approximate time of death and whether a body has been moved, because after the blood has settled it stays put—it does not "resettle" when the body is moved. If the body has been moved, then the blood will not be in a logical position.

loan shark

A person who lends money at usurious interest rates.

A shark is perceived as a savage, ruthless beast that never stops eating. It is no small wonder that someone who lends money at exorbitant rates (interest can be 5 percent a week) is characterized this way.

The term first emerged in the United States in the 1920s, but its origin appears to be German (*schurke*) and goes back to the late 1500s.

There never seems an end to people who want to feed loan sharks, and most sharks do an excellent business. Ideally, many big-time loan sharks prefer that businessmen get in trouble paying the loan back, because usually the business has been put up as collateral.

locker

The heart.

loid

A stiff, thin piece of plastic used to disengage simple door locks.

The latch on a cheap lock is spring actuated, meaning that it locks in and out of position depending on whether the key is inserted in the cylinder and turned. To open it, all one has to do is push the loid between the latch and the strike and pry the latch out of strike far enough so the door can be pushed open.

A loid will not work on a dead bolt lock, which is not spring actuated. A key must be used to turn the cylinder to pull the latch from the plate.

Loid is a shortened version of celluloid, or film strip. The term has been around since the late 1930s. "You said you could use a loid. Let's see you open that door" (M. Proctor, *Man in Ambush,* 1938).

See also *PICK MAN.*

LoJack

An electronic system for tracking stolen cars.

LoJack—manufactured by a Dedham, Massachusetts, company of the same name—is the name for an electronic tracking system that involves installing hidden transmitters in cars that emit signals to receivers installed in police cars and helicopters. As long as the cars are within range of the police receiving units, vehicle recovery is possible.

Police departments in nine states are currently equipped with the devices. The company does not charge the police for the receivers, but charges $595 to install a transmitter in a car. Insurance companies give 15 percent discounts on annual premiums to vehicle owners who have these transmitters installed. Thus far the system is said to be 95 percent effective, failing only where stolen cars go out of range or where the transmitters are damaged.

loo

In the New York area, a police lieutenant.

William Caunitz, himself once a lieutenant in the NYPD, provided one of the more famous uses for this term in his novel *One Police Plaza*. A homicide investigator calls a lieutenant, rousing him from bed:

" 'Hey loo,' he said, 'we got a little problem.' "

The little problem was a priest who had suffered a heart attack while copulating with a prostitute.

lookout file

A file, maintained by the State Department, of people who may not be eligible for passports.

The names of people with questionable or criminal backgrounds are kept in this file. If someone listed applies for a passport, a more than routine investigation is conducted to determine eligibility. If the file is "flagged," it means that a governmental agency must be immediately notified of the application.

loused

See *BUGGED.*

low, low sick

Someone who is in very poor physical condition.

This usually applies to someone who has been shot, stabbed, or otherwise physically assaulted.

LSD

Lysergic acid diethylamide, a hallucinogenic drug.

Commonly called acid, LSD is usually sold in tablet form, thin squares of gelatin ("windowpanes"), or impregnated paper known as "blotter acid." It is taken orally (*DROPPED*), with the average effective dose being from 30 to 50 micrograms. Higher doses last 10 to 12 hours, but tolerance develops rapidly. LSD is not regarded as a physically addictive drug; whether it is psychologically addictive is moot.

LSD is produced by lysergic acid, itself produced from the ergot fungus that grows on rye, or from lysergic acid amide, a chemical found in morning glory seeds. The drug was first synthesized in 1938, but its psychotomimetic effects were not learned until 1943 when a chemist accidentally ingested some and went on the first documented *TRIP.* The light intensified; he experienced vertigo; and when he closed his eyes, he saw extraordinarily vivid and colorful images. The trip lasted about two hours.

LSD became very popular in America in the 1960s, and is commonly thought to have originated in America in the Haight Ashbury section of San Francisco, where it became one of the most commonly used drugs and a symbol of hippie culture. But it was well known in other cultures and countries before it came to the states. "I dropped my first acid in Paris," said R. Bronsteen in *Hippies Handbook* (1960).

As time went by and the hippie culture faded, so did LSD. Conventional wisdom stated that it was a very dangerous drug, able to produce long-lasting negative effects, though this has not been definitively established.

LSD has been used licitly and illicitly. Because the chemicals in it bear close relationship to those inside the brain, it has been used as a tool to try to alter the brain and to explore mental illness. The fantasies produced by its ingestion mimic certain aspects of psychosis. In a sense, those who go on a trip are experiencing a form of psychosis.

LSD is now back in favor, being commonly available on the *STREET*. The amount per dose bought on the street varies greatly.

Acid is by far the most common expression for LSD, but there are plenty of others:

A
animal
back breakers (LSD and strychnine)
barrels
battery acid
beast
big D
black acid (LSD, or LSD in combination with PCP)
black star
black sunshine
black tabs
blotter
blotter acid
blotter cube
blue acid
blue barrels
blue chairs
blue cheers
blue heaven

blue microdot
blue mist
blue moons
blue vials
brown bombers
brown dots
California sunshine
cap
chief
chocolate chips
Cid
coffee
conductor
contact lens
crackers
crystal tea
cube
cupcakes
D
deeds
domes

dots
double dome
electric Kool-Aid
fields
flash
flat blues
ghost
god's flesh
golden dragon
goofys
grape parfait
green single dome
green wedge
grey shields
hats
Hawaiian sunshine
hawk
haze
head light
heavenly blue
instant zen
L
LBJ
lason sa daga
lens
lime acid
little smoke
logor
Lucy in the sky with diamonds
mellow yellow
Mickeys
microdot
mighty Quinn
mind detergent
one way
optical illusion
orange barrels

orange cubes
orange haze
orange micro
orange wedges
Owsley
Owsley's acid
pane
paper acid
peace
peace tables
pearly gates
pebbles
pink blotters
pink robots
pink wedges
pink witches
potato
pure love
purple barrels
purple flats
purple haze
purple hearts
purple ozoline
recycle
royal blues
Russian sickles
Sandoz
sacrament
smears
snowmen
squirrel
strawberry fields
sugar
sugar lumps
sunshine
tabs
taillights

the goose	white lightning
the hawk	white Owsley's
ticket	window glass
twenty-five	windowpane
vodka acid	yellow
wedding bells	yellow dimples
wedge	yellow sunshine
white dust	zen

ludes

Short for Quaaludes, a brand name for methaqualone, a popular nonbarbiturate sedative and hypnotic drug.

Ludes are characterized as barbiturates and have the same effects, including loss of motor control, hence they're also known as *wallbangers.*

See also *BARBS.*

lush worker

Someone who steals from sleeping riders on subway trains.

These are thieves who roam city subways looking for people who have fallen asleep so they can steal their wallets, bags, whatever. While "lush" implies that the victim is drunk, police view the practice more broadly. "Any sleeping person robbed on a train is deemed a lush which has been worked," says author Jim Dwyer in *Subway Lives* (1991).

lustmurderer

A kind of *SERIAL MURDERER* who kills someone and then conducts a "mutilating attack or displacement of the breasts, rectum, and genitals" on the victims, as stated by FBI agents Robert R. Hazlewood and John E. Douglas in the April 1980 issue of *FBI Law Enforcement* bulletin.

The FBI says that it is the mutilation done to the body after death that separates lustmurder from "sadistic homicide," in which the mutilation occurs prior to death. According to the FBI there are two types of lustmurderer: *ORGANIZED* and *DISORGANIZED.* Far more dangerous are the organized ones, because their attacks are much more highly structured and planned than the disorganized, and they are far more devious.

Lustmurderers would seem to be a modern phenomenon, but they are not. One of the most famous lustmurderers of all time was Jack the Ripper, who killed five prostitutes in London a little over a century ago. The popular conception is that Jack stabbed the women and cut their throats. In fact, post mortem mutilation to the bodies was vast, including the removal of organs. It was this opening up of the victims that made investigators of the day theorize that he had surgical training: The mutilation was carried out with some precision.

Agents in the *BSU* coined the term lustmurderer. "Lust" in this term has more to do with bloodlust than sex.

Some lustmurderers are necrophiles—they are obsessed with corpses and erotically stimulated by them. Edmund Kemper, an organized lustmurderer who killed six coeds on the West Coast, had no sex with his victims until after the murders. He then took parts of the body into the shower and used them as masturbatory aids. Henry Lee Lucas also killed his victims before having sex with them. When a police officer asked why he never had sex with a living victim, his answer was "I like peace and quiet."

There are various theories on why such sexual activity and mutilation occurs. One particularly plausible explanation is that the lustmurderer is acting out fantasies of control and power. You have things totally your way when a victim is dead.

M

made man

A full member of the *MAFIA*.

Only Italians can become mafiosi, though outside talent is welcome. For example, Meyer Lansky, one of the most active and brilliant criminals ever, allegedly made the Mafia a ton of money but never became a made man.

Members are "made" in the sense that they "have it made" financially. Belonging to the Mafia ensures a good living—as long as one follows family rules.

In order to become a made man, one has to demonstrate absolute loyalty, which may even involve taking someone's life.

See also *BUTTON MAN, MAKE YOUR BONES, WANNABES,* and *WISE GUY.*

Mafia

A secret criminal organization with members of Italian descent.

The term Mafia refers to more than just a gang of criminals. It has a long history in Sicily, where it emerged, and referred to a variety of things, such as defiance of authority, manhood, loyalty, and a state of mind.

The Mafia is a structured organization much like an army. Each member has a specific role. Of course, breaking Mafia rules can result in sanctions far more severe than an army would normally impose.

See also *BUTTON MAN, MADE MAN, THE MOB,* and *WISE GUY.*

maggot

A criminal.

This is a favorite term that cops use to describe someone who is despicable and parasitical, such as a *DRUG DEALER*.

Despite their repulsiveness, maggots are nothing more than fly larvae. Flies deposit eggs on decaying flesh; the wormlike larvae hatch from the eggs, feed on the flesh, and eventually transform into adult flies. This cycle of propagation continues to repeat itself, and the host (dead body) will be swarming with flies in all stages of development. Because this process normally occurs over a set period of time, depending on the fly species, investigators can often use the developmental stages of the maggots to help establish time of death.

See also *MUTT*.

mail cover

Photocopies of the front and back of mail, made by the Postal Authorities and used to trace a missing person.

To get a *LEAD* on a person's whereabouts, governmental agencies may empower the post office to photocopy the front and back of all mail destined for a specific address that the missing person is likely to write to.

mainline

To inject drugs, usually into the arm.

This is one of the most common ways to refer to intravenous injection of illegal drugs, but there are several others, including the following:

blackjack
backtrack (allow blood to flow back into the needle during injection)
backup (to prepare a vein for injection)
bang
bingo
blow a fix (injection misses the vein and is wasted)
blow the vein

boost
boot
bridge or bring up (ready a vein for injection)
burn the main line
draw up
dropper
fire
flag (appearance of blood in a vein)
geezer

geezin a bit of dee gee	laugh and scratch
go into a sewer	miss
gravy	sewer (vein into which a drug is
gutter (vein into which drug is	injected)
injected)	shoot up
hit the main line	shot
hit the pit	skin popping (injecting drugs
hitting up	under the skin)
jab	slam
job	tie
jolt	

make

To identify someone.

This is a very common term among police: "Did you make him?" (Did you identify him?)

make a canoe

To do an autopsy.

In the simplest terms, during an autopsy a body is laid on a stainless steel table, cut open, and the organs are removed, leaving a hollowed-out shell, just as one might make a canoe using the ancient technique of scooping out the interior matter of a log with an adze and leaving a floatable shell. Like so many terms in law enforcement, it is grisly but humorous.

See also *OPEN HER/HIM UP, POST,* and *PROTOCOL.*

make a play

In prison, to attempt to deceive someone.

make-believe cops

Volunteer police officers.

This is a term used by regular police officers. Unpaid volunteers for police departments throughout the country perform important functions, such as traffic duties, that free regular police for other duties. Make-believe police may be in uniform and look like regular police, but there is a fundamental difference: Volunteers do not carry guns and are not empowered to use *DEADLY FORCE.*

make your bones

In *MAFIA* parlance, to carry out a murder for the first time.

The phrase refers to the idea that in murdering someone, you make a skeleton, or bones.

When an individual becomes a *MADE MAN,* or Mafia member, a sign of absolute loyalty is required, and killing someone is one way to give it. One of the more well-known uses of the phrase occurred in the move *Godfather II* when Moe Green, the operator of a Las Vegas hotel/gambling casino pointed out to Don Corleone (the Godfather) that he, Green, "made his bones" when Corleone was just a kid. Green, of course, was shortly made into bones.

man (the)

The police.

In ghettos and on *THE STREET* in general, the most common term for the police is The Man. It imputes an almost regal presence, judge, jury, and executioner all in one.

See also *COP.*

maricon

A homosexual.

This Spanish slang term is used by both Hispanic and non-Hispanic police.

marijuana

See *POT.*

mass murder

The act of murdering a number of people at the same time.

While the general sense of the phrase is the simultaneous murdering of a lot of people, Vernon Geberth, who investigated over 5,000 homicides while head of the Bronx homicide squad, fine-tuned the definition in his book *Practical Homicide Investigation.* Geberth wrote that mass murder must involve "four or more victims during a single event at one location." He breaks this down into what he characterizes as "classic," which involves a single *PERPE-TRATOR* killing four or more people over a short period of time. The "family-member murder" involves the murder of three or more people within that time frame as well as the killer taking his or her own life. A "family killing" is "four or more family members killed by a family member who does not commit suicide."

Many people confuse serial and mass murder. Essentially, the difference is that *SERIAL MURDERERS* kill people one by one at different times and places, whereas mass murderers kill a number of people in one place at one time.

Modern mass murder in America seems to have started on September 6, 1949, in Camden, New Jersey. On that day a World War II vet named Howard Unruh, dressed in a snappy suit and bow tie and carrying a PPK Walther, a gun he had gotten while in the army, calmly walked up and down Riverside Road shooting people at point-blank range. He killed thirteen people and wounded many more. Almost miraculously, Unruh was captured alive; and he is still ensconced in Trenton State Hospital for the Criminally Insane.

One especially scary aspect of mass murders is that they seem to occur in clusters, as if the actions of one person gave ideas to someone else. Some psychiatrists believe this actually happens.

maytag

Prisoner who is not strong enough to protect himself who arranges to be taken care of by a stronger inmate in return for "favors."

An inmate under the protection of another may grant him not only sexual favors but also housekeeping chores, including doing his laundry. Hence the term maytag, which is a popular brand of washing machine.

See also *BACKER, JAILHOUSE TURNOUT,* and *JOCKER.*

ME

Common abbreviation for medical examiner, a physician who determines the cause of death.

The ME must by law be in attendance at the crime scene of deaths due to suicide, accident, or homicide; any death under suspicious circumstances; sudden death when health was good; and convict deaths.

The ME takes charge of any crime scene he or she is called to, and the body may not be removed without the ME's permission. The body is then taken to the morgue, where an autopsy is performed.

Some police departments have a coroner come to the scene instead of the ME. In some cases, this is merely a political appointee who moves the body to a funeral home. An autopsy must be done by a qualified person, and the coroner is sometimes as qualified as the ME—the names are just different.

It is well known that there are competent and incompetent MEs. Many homicide victims have been buried without the true cause of death being known. Determining cause of death can be a difficult, subtle exercise, particularly if a killer is skillful in hiding it. In the 1970s, for example, a doctor in New Jersey, dubbed Dr. X by the media, used an almost undetectable poison, curare, to kill people.

meateater

A police officer who takes cash bribes.

This term was first used at the Knapp Commission Hearings on Corruption in the 1960s by an NYPD detective named William Phillips, himself a meateater and murderer. It describes the worst kind of *DIRTY* cop, the one who looks the other way no matter what illegal activity is going on. The term is no longer widely used.

See also *GRASSEATER.*

meat wagon

Vehicle used to transport dead to the morgue; also known as a *morgue wagon.*

mechanic

1. A contract killer.
    See *HIT MAN.*
2. An enforcer in the NYPD. This term surfaced in the 1993 Mollen Commission hearings on corruption in the NYPD. A beefy cop spoke of how he would beat people up—"tune 'em up"—if they weren't cooperating in the bribery scams being perpetrated by the cops.

medical examiner

See *ME.*

meet
> See *SIT-DOWN*.

mentally aided
> See *EDP*.

Mexican lightning
> Arson.
>
> This is the California equivalent to *JEWISH LIGHTNING* in the East. The implication is that Mexicans are the main offenders when it comes to arson.

Mickey Finn
> A very strong alcoholic drink or one spiked with knockout drops intended to render a person helpless.
>
> The origin of Mickey Finn is unfortunately not known, but it was well established by the 1920s as something that meant both spiking someone's drink and getting someone drunk.
>
> "I got a bottle of brandy. . . . He was lit up . . . but I shot him a few more Mickey Finns (double drinks) into him" (M. C. Sharpe, *Chicago Man,* 1928). "But he never slipped an obstreperous customer the croton oil Mickey Finn of the modern night club" (*American Mercury Magazine,* March 1936).

milk powder
> A substance used to cut, or dilute, heroin.

Mirandize
> To warn a suspect before questioning that he or she has the right to speak with a lawyer and has protections against self-incrimination.
>
> The term was named for Ernesto O. Miranda, a man who was arrested without his rights being read to him. He filed suit against the state of Arizona, and he was ultimately victorious in the U.S. Supreme Court, where his case was linked with four others. The decision has had a profound effect on law enforcement procedures. Before making an arrest, every officer is now required to read the suspect his rights under the Miranda ruling, and if the suspect is not properly Mirandized by the officer—which sometimes happens— the suspect is sure to be set free by the courts.

misdemeanor

A crime of lesser gravity than a *FELONY.*

Misdemeanors include crimes such as disorderly conduct, indecent behavior, and shoplifting of merchandise under a certain value.

missionary

See *DRUG DEALER.*

MO

Acronym for modus operandi (mode of operating).

The MO is very important in helping police determine if a crime was committed by a particular criminal. For example, if a series of robberies are committed, and the burglar picks a particular kind of house (say, mansions), and operates at certain times of the day (say, late afternoon), and gains entry after cleverly disarming an alarm system, and takes certain kinds of goods (such as silverware), then police can see a clear MO and can try to predict where the criminal might show up next.

To a degree, the investigator profiles the perpetrator to come up with the MO, but it is not *PROFILING* in the sense that describes the method developed by the *BSU.* Profiling creates a detailed psychological portrait of the perpetrator, while the MO focuses mainly on the method.

mob (the)

A unit of organized crime.

The mob is a common term that all kinds of law enforcement entities use in describing organized crime. It seems to date back to the 1920s, a truncated version of the seventeenth-century Latin *mobile,* itself condensed from *mobile vulgus,* or a moving crowd of excited people—rabble.

See also *MAFIA.*

mole

A spy who is employed by the people he or she is spying on.

In the last few years mole has come into popular consciousness, but it has been around quite awhile. There is some misunderstanding about the little animal whose name is used so libelously. It does burrow into the ground, but this doesn't make it blind nor is it born blind. It just has small eyes.

Molotov cocktail

A homemade incendiary device.

A Molotov cocktail is constructed by filling a bottle with two-thirds gasoline and one-third oil. A gasoline-soaked rag is stuffed into the bottle to serve as a fuse. A cork is pushed in place. The fuse is then lit and the bottle is thrown. When it hits, the bottle breaks and the gas ignites and is very difficult to extinguish.

money laundering

The process of concealing illegally earned money by converting it to other assets.

Drug dealing produces large amounts of cash—$40 billion to $50 billion a year—and the people involved face the problems of concealing the money, explaining to the IRS where it all came from, and paying taxes on it. It's also heavy and bulky, easily stolen, and earns no interest unless invested. This is where money laundering comes in. Money launderers and traffickers make the money "clean" in a variety of ways.

One way is to convert it into money orders and cashier's checks, which allow immediate payment with no questions asked. Cash is also unloaded at gambling casinos and by buying relatively liquid assets such as gold, jewelry, rare or expensive coins, autos, boats, planes, and communications equipment.

Of course, launderers can also deposit the money in a bank, but must avoid a situation in which the bank reports the transaction to the IRS, something it is required to do by U.S. law for any deposit of $10,000 and over. This is accomplished in a variety of ways, including *SMURFING*, bribery, and coercion.

Smurfing is the process of structuring deposits so that they are under $10,000 each; more sophisticated smurfing involves having more than one account in the same bank.

Bank officials may be bribed to look the other way when traffickers make large deposits—and the bribes can indeed be large. Between 1980 and 1991, officials of the Great American Bank in Miami were paid $94 million to look the other way.

153

When smurfing and bribery fail, there's always coercion. Threatening bank officials with bodily harm can be quite effective.

One of the largest money-laundering operations ever was *La Mina* (The Mine), which processed millions of dollars a year for the Colombian drug cartels. In 1989 the U.S. government tracked the path of the money. Around $600 million from cocaine sales was packed in boxes labeled JEWELRY and sent by armored car to Ropex, a jewelry maker in Los Angeles. At Ropex, the cash was counted and deposited in banks that filed the CTRs (Currency Transaction Reports) with the IRS. Few suspicions were raised, even by the immense amounts of money transferred, because the jewelry/gold business is often done in cash. Ropex then transferred the money by wire (see *WIRE TRANSFERS*) to New York banks in payment for fictitious gold bought from Ronel, a "dummy" gold bullion business. Ronel sent the "gold" (actually bars of lead painted to look like gold) to Ropex. Ronel then completed the transaction by transferring the $600 million from American banks to banks in South America where the Colombian cartel could access the funds.

See also *CASAS DE CAMBIO* and *CMIR*.

morgue wagon

See *MEAT WAGON*.

mother

See *DRUG DEALER*.

mother's helper

Valium, a tranquilizer used to relieve anxiety and tension.

Mr. Stranger Danger

Stranger who commits random sex crimes; stranger who abducts and murders a child.

Many sex crimes against children and adults are committed by people who know the victims, even if only in a passing way. But some predators prey on people they don't know, mostly selecting them at random. A sex crimes investigator in the Chicago PD defined it in Connie Fletcher's *What Cops Know*. "Mr. Stranger Danger—Mr. Unknown, Mr. Abductor or Invader of some type, the guy who drags you off the street into the car or drags you off the street into the gangway, the guy who climbs into your bedroom window. Somebody you have no previous experience with, and it kind of indicates random selection."

mug book

Book containing photos of known criminals.

mugger

Someone who robs people on the street.

The word probably arises from the term "mug," which in the nineteenth century referred to someone who was slow and innocent and somewhat doltish, and from this to a mugger, someone who would prey on mugs. This sense of the word was used in the 1865 book *Four Years in Succesia* by J. H. Brown: "The muggers, like most bullies and ruffians, manifested a fine discrimination respecting the party they attacked, those they thought they could rob with little resistance and entire impunity."

mule

1. A carrier of illegal drugs.

   Mules may carry drugs inside a prison, out on the street, or internationally, and they will go to fantastic lengths to get the drug from one place to another.

   In prison, where the most common contraband is drugs, the drug often is inserted in a balloon that is then inserted in the rectum (see *KEISTER STASH*).

   Women traveling internationally will carry drugs in their vaginas. And some people (called swallowers) will swallow balloons filled with drugs. Sometimes the bags or balloons break, killing the mule.

   One of the more bizarre methods of carrying cocaine internationally was used by a person who had one pound of cocaine—half a *KEY*—surgically implanted under the skin of his thighs. The cocaine was divided into four one-inch square packages weighing a quarter-pound each; two packages were implanted in each thigh.

2. A professional car thief.

   Also called a *puller.*

3. Person who carries money generated by drugs or gambling.

    Huge amounts of cash are generated by the drug business, and mules carry it to various locations for laundering.

    See also *MONEY LAUNDERING*.

murder book (the)

In Los Angeles, a record of all data and photographs compiled by the district attorney's office as it investigates a homicide.

    This term came into the public consciousness during the murder trial of O. J. Simpson. Simpson's lawyer, Robert Shapiro, stated at one point that the district attorney was to furnish him with the murder book.

mutt

Police term for a person of very poor character.

    Though the word is often associated with dogs, Hugh Rawson in *Wicked Words* points out that mutt is really a shortened version of muttonhead, a sheep.

    Notwithstanding the traditional use of the term to describe an ugly woman, when police call someone a mutt, they are not only referring to the person's look, but are implying that the person is of mixed parentage—a bastard. Mutt is among the most common terms used by cops to describe *BAD GUYS*.

    See also *MAGGOT*.

MVA

Motor vehicle accident.

    See also *FATAL*.

mystery

Any murder that has gone unsolved for at least forty-eight hours.

    Most homicides are solved within the first forty-eight hours, usually because there is a well-known connection. The murderer may have been someone close to the victim, possibly a family member. The murder might have also had many witnesses, such as in a bar fight. Interviewing the witnesses quickly turns up likely suspects; or, in a drug-related killing, the *PERP* might be known.

    If a homicide goes beyond the forty-eight hours, however, it is characterized as a mystery, also known as a *whodunit* or *puzzle* (depending on the police department), and becomes progressively more difficult to solve. It probably means that the victim didn't know the killer, making it difficult for the police to make any connection. So they search for a stranger, often with negative results. Enlarging the problem these days is the emergence of the *SERIAL MURDERER*, who will kill at random without motive, typically traveling across state lines making apprehension very difficult.

According to FBI statistics, most of the murders committed today are by serial murderers.

See also *GROUNDER.*

N

nail

To arrest.

narco

A detective in the narcotics bureau of a police department.

Working as a narco is very difficult in terms of the temptations present—that is, immense amounts of used currency available for stealing. When scandal shows up in various police entities across America, drugs are invariably involved, simply because that's where the big money is. Some cops become drug dealers, but most who steal will do so at the scene of a raid, or perhaps at a homicide in which money is found either at the location or on the deceased. A few "samples" may be taken.

Narcs (or narcos) are always aware that they may be set up. If *IAD* investigators suspect someone of thievery, they know that all they have to do is plant money where the suspected *DIRTY* cop will be and let nature take its course. For example, one narco was trapped at the home of a drug dealer who had been arrested. The narco was told to search the place, and he did, finding about $5,000 in a cheese container in the refrigerator. He took the money and was promptly arrested.

The job is also difficult in terms of the kinds of people one deals with. "These are not upstanding citizens," says one cop. "They're shitbirds."

NCAVC

National Center for the Analysis of Violent Crime.

This national clearing house of information is operated by the FBI to help local police jurisdictions solve cases involving violent *OFFENDERS*.

See also *PROFILING*.

needle freak

Someone who injects drugs with hypodermic needles.

needle sharing

Using hypodermic needles that others have used to inject drugs.

This practice carries high risk because the AIDS virus is often transmitted through the sharing of needles or syringes or other equipment. Drug users who are HIV positive commonly frequent *SHOOTING GALLERIES* where needle sharing is a common practice.

"net worth" investigation

An investigation into the finances of someone to determine if they are living beyond their means.

A "net worth" investigation is a common way to catch *DIRTY* police officers. A surprising number are not circumspect enough to live within their means, and they therefore attract attention and become a target. "When someone on the job is making forty grand a year," says one prosecutor, "and he has a boat that looks like a yacht and a Lamborghini in his driveway, you start wondering."

nickel

1. Five dollars.
2. Five years in prison.

nickel bag

Five dollars' worth of drugs in one container.

nightstick

See *BATON*.

non compos mentis

Mentally disturbed.

This is an older police term, on the level of *EDP* (emotionally disturbed person) or *mentally aided,* but is still used occasionally. Translated from Latin it literally means "Not master of one's mind."

nutsack

Prison parlance for manhood or courage.

O

observe

To see.

Police never say that they see something, only that they observe it.

OD

See *HOT SHOT*.

offender

The perpetrator of a crime.

Offender is typical of the way police euphemize things, particularly in public pronouncements. An offender could be someone who runs a red light or a person who is a mass murderer.

The term derives from the legal terminology of committing an offense, which is another way to describe breaking the law.

offshore banks

Financial institutions in foreign countries that have bank secrecy laws and are often tax havens for the larcenous.

See also *MONEY LAUNDERING*.

OG

An "original gangster," a veteran gangster who has earned a place of status in the gang by dint of accomplishments and experience.

one (the)

In East Los Angeles, the police.

This often takes the place of *FIVE-O*.

See also *COP.*

on ice

In jail.

on the job

To be on active duty as a police officer.

The term may apply in a general sense to anyone who works in law enforcement, but it is more closely associated with regular police rather than specialized forces such as the FBI or Immigration and Naturalization.

If one cop suspects that another person is a cop, the question is likely to be "You on the job?"

on the nod

Sleepy from taking drugs.

Some drugs, such as speed, put people into overdrive, but many drugs make people relax to the point where they feel like going to sleep.

on the pad

Taking regular bribes as a police officer.

Taking bribes was once considered business as usual for the many police departments in America, and just about everyone would be involved, from the commanding officers down to the lowest *BEAT* officers (when you think about it, it's hard to imagine widespread bribery existing without the complicity of higher-ups). Payments were made by bookies, madams, and bootleggers to allow business to go on as usual. At specified intervals, usually weekly, payments would be collected and distributed. If you were the kind of officer who refused the payments, you were immediately regarded with distrust. It was take the booty—or resign.

The most common phrase for this systematic bribe-taking was to be "on the pad." "The gamblers of the city paid off the policemen on a regular monthly basis after they had been placed on what is called 'on the pad' " (*New York Times,* October 19, 1972).

The phrase, still used, arises out of the word "padder," which in the seventeenth century described a highway robber or purse-taker. The "padder" was a thief on the "pad," or street.

on the tin

Getting a free meal or services because you are a police officer.

This practice used to be much more common. It was more or less expected that police officers didn't have to pay for meals or services. The business community was never asked if they liked the practice, but it's hard to see how they could.

Today such minor corruption is much less evident in PDs across the country. For one thing there is an increased awareness that it is morally wrong, and for another there is much more fear of being discovered, particularly since the proliferation of video cameras.

See also *GRASSEATER.*

on vacation

Gang euphemism for someone who is in jail.

open her/him up

To perform an autopsy.

When an autopsy is performed, usually by the *CORONER* or *ME,* the body is literally opened up with knives and saws to gain access to the internal organs. "Open him up" is the way many cops refer to it. "Yeah," one homicide investigator said, speaking of a female decedent, "we're going to follow that up as soon as we open her up."

See also *MAKE A CANOE, POST,* and *PROTOCOL.*

Oreo team

Both black and white criminals or police officers who work together.

The reference, of course, is to the Oreo cookie, which was described in 1979 in *Mother Wit* by A. Dundes as a "cookie which has two disc-shaped chocolate wafers separated by sugar cream filling."

The term is more likely to be used to describe criminals, but has also been used to describe a police team of both black and white officers. In the *Lethal Weapon* movies, for example, actors Danny Glover and Mel Gibson formed an Oreo team, though, strictly speaking, one would need another black person to truly parallel the cookie analogy.

Originally, when the term arose in the late 1960s, Oreo was used in a derisive fashion to describe a black man who was black on the outside but white on the inside.

organized murderer

A type of *LUSTMURDERER*.

The organized murderer plans his offense, targets strangers, exercises power and control, and is devious in the extreme. The organized murderer will also blend easily into the fabric of society, displaying enough charm and personableness to fool the public. These murderers are extremely dangerous.

See also *DISORGANIZED MURDERER*.

organ trophies

Organs that some killers will remove from bodies and take with them.

This practice is most common among *LUSTMURDERERS,* who frequently open up victims *POST MORTEM* (after death), examine their organs, and sometimes take them to be used later. For example, Ed Gein (pronounced Gain), the real-life person that the character of Norman Bates was based on in the film *Psycho,* regularly removed women's organs and wore them.

ounce dealer

See *DOPE DEALER*.

outfit (the)

1. A syringe and hypodermic needle used to inject drugs.
2. An organized crime gang in Chicago.

out of pocket

To be in violation of the unwritten prisoner code of fair play.

outs

Los Angeles gang term describing the state of being free, not in prison or detention.

overamped

See *AMPED*.

P

package

See *BLIZZARD*.

packing

1. To be armed, usually with a gun.

    The term seems to be a shortened version of "pistol packing," as in "pistol-packing momma." Packing has also been used as a general term for carrying other kinds of weapons ("How do you suppose we're going to stop a mob of eight dagger-packing Greeks?"—Eric Ambler, *Dark Frontier*), but it is most closely associated with guns.

2. Carrying contraband in prison.

paperwork

A general term police use to describe the variety of reports they are required to submit.

Paperwork is the bane of a police officer's existence, but it is required. Much of the business of investigating crime will end up in the courts, and written records—a "trail of paper"—is required.

In general, police officers struggle with writing reports. The classic image of a detective sitting at a battered desk and hunt-and-pecking his way through a report is not far from the truth.

pat down

A very light search of a prisoner or suspect involving feeling the outside of his/her body and clothing.

See also *"ASSUME THE POSITION"* and *STRIP SEARCH*.

pattern rapist

See *SERIAL RAPIST.*

PC

Police commissioner.

In *PDs*, the highest ranking official.

For most police officers, the PC is on the level of a divine being, and to be called to his office is a rattling experience. An Albuquerque, New Mexico, policeman was once asked if he were more afraid to go down a dark alley after a *PERP* than into the PC's office. He claimed to be more fearful of the PC's office and explained why: "It's the PC," he said, "who allows you to go down those alleys in the first place."

PCP

Street name for phencyclidine and related drugs.

PCP is one of the nastiest drugs around and is banned in the United States for use in humans. PCP was introduced in the 1950s as an anesthetic, and for a time it was used on animals under the brand name Sernylan, but production stopped in 1978 soon after it was found to have bad side effects.

In its pure form PCP is a white powder, but for the street it is diluted and may be any color from tan to brown. It is commonly sprinkled on cigarettes filled with marijuana, oregano, parsley, or mint and smoked.

Its effect can vary greatly, but the most common physiological reaction is a blank stare and random, rapid eye movements. Walking may be exaggerated, hearing distorted, and vision impaired—the world can start to look like images in a fun house mirror. Numbness and slurred speech can also result.

Psychological reactions can also vary. A mild effect may be to invest the user with a sense of superiority and invulnerability. But PCP can also produce tremendous anxiety, causing the user to anxiously wait for disaster to strike. It may also make users paranoid and hostile. Indeed, PCP has the dubious distinction of being better than any other drug at simulating schizophrenia. It is regarded to be as dangerous as *CRACK.*

PCP and angel dust are the most common names for phencyclidine, but it has many other slang terms on *THE STREET*, including the following:

ace
amoeba
angel mist
animal track
animal tranquilizer
aurora borealis
beam me up Scotty
  (PCP and crack)
black acid (PCP and
  LSD)
black whack
bohd
busy bee
butt naked
CJ
Cadillac
cannibinol
cigarrode cristal
clicker (PCP and
  crack)
Columbo
cozmo's
crystal
crystal joint
cyclones
DMT
DOA
Detroit pink
devil's dust
dust
dust of angels
dusted parsley

el diablito (PCP,
  marijuana,
  cocaine, and
  heroin)
elephant
embalming fluid
earth
fuel
goon
goon dust
gorilla biscuits
green
green leaves
HCP
hinkley
hog
horse
horse tranquilizer
jet fuel
juice
KJ
kaps
killer
KW
LBJ
log
loveboat
lovely
magic dust
mist
monkey dust
monkey tranquilizer

more
new magic
niebla
ozone
P-funk (PCP and
  crack)
peace pill
pits
polvo
rocket fuel
STP
scaffle
Shermans
Sherms
soma
space base (PCP and
  crack)
space dust (PCP and
  crack)
squirrel (PCP and
  marijuana sprin-
  kled with cocaine
  and smoked)
taking a cruise
tic tac
wack
white horizon
white powder
yerba mala (PCP
  and marijuana)
zombie
zoom

PD
Police department.

pedestrian stop
Police stopping a pedestrian for any reason, but particularly stopping a person who seems to be acting suspiciously; also known as *field interrogation.*

Any time a police officer stops a pedestrian under suspicious circumstances, the situation can be considered hazardous. Such stops have more than occasionally resulted in gunplay.

See also *FELONY STOP.*

pedigree
The character and quality of a suspect or witness.

peewee
Five dollars' worth of *CRACK.*

pen
Short for penitentiary.

This is a favorite police word for prison that dates back at least to 1620: "He's taken to the tower's strength. . . . We have him in a pen, he cannot escape us" (*Double Marriage,* Fletcher and Massinger).

See also *BOX, CAN,* and *COOLER.*

pen register
Recording device that can be attached to a telephone to record the phone numbers of calls made to that particular phone.

Up until the early 1980s, pen registers simply recorded the telephone numbers of outgoing calls. The device would be connected to a sort of teletype at the phone company's central office, and a pin would punch long sheets of paper with the numbers called.

Today pen registers are much more sophisticated and can record both incoming and outgoing calls.

See also *BUG, TAP,* and *WIRE.*

Pepsi habit
See *CHIP.*

perp

A criminal; short for *PERPETRATOR.*

perpetrator

Someone who commits a crime.

This is one of the most common law enforcement terms. If a criminal event occurs and an official of a *PD* appears on TV, he or she will surely talk about the perpetrator involved. In private conversation with peers or others, police use a shortened version, *PERP.*

The term goes back to the sixteenth century and was used in a criminalistic sense even then.

perp walk

The orchestrated showing by police of a *SUSPECT* or *PERP* to the media.

For publicity, police commonly arrange to have a perp or suspect escorted past the media at a designated time, usually from a building entrance to a waiting vehicle. If the suspect/perp is important enough, he or she will be walked around the block, followed by a horde of media. This is called "parading the perp."

petechial hemorrhages

Burst blood vessels in the linings of the eyelids, which mean that the decedent suffered asphyxial death.

When air supply is constricted, blood rushes to the surface of the skin and petechial hemorrhages, or petechiae, usually result. To a homicide investigator, petechiae becomes as familiar as his or her own name.

phat

Black lingo meaning cool, with it, *FRESH.*

The term might be a play on the word fat, meaning full, fat, and sassy, all together.

photo lineup

See *MUG BOOK.*

physical evidence

Evidence found at a crime scene that may prove conclusively whether a person is guilty or innocent of a particular crime.

pick man

Someone who picks locks to gain unlawful entry.

Picking locks to burglarize a place has been going on at least since the sixteenth century.

See also *LOID.*

pickpocket

See *DIP.*

piece

1. A handgun.
2. One ounce of a drug.

pigeon

1. A victim of a con artist.

    The word comes from the Latin *pipere,* "to cheep," and it originally referred to a young bird. Since around the sixteenth century, however, it has more or less meant simpleton, someone who is easily fooled. "It is the pigeons who lose the most . . . perhaps the pigeons are not bad players either, but simply not acclimated to John Huston's presence" (*New York Times,* August 23, 1983).

2. Intermediaries who, for a set price, steer drug *TRAFFICKERS* to *MONEY LAUNDERERS.*

3. An informer. See *STOOL PIGEON.*

pigeon drop

A confidence game.

This *CON* is as old as the hills, but it still works. It begins with a pair of hustlers befriending someone. The con artists and their new-found friend will then have the good fortune to discover a bag containing a sum of money. They will all agree that the *PIGEON* will hold the bag until they're sure the owner is not coming back to claim it. If the owner doesn't return, they agree to divide the money among them.

The pigeon agrees, whereupon the *CON MEN* ask him to provide them with some money to make sure he won't run away with the money in the bag. Once the pigeon does this, the con men distract him so they can either grab the money from the bag or switch it with an identical bag containing strips of newspaper. Then they depart.

pimp

Someone who supplies women for prostitution.

The popular image of the pimp dressed like a rhinestone cowboy and driving a Cadillac has pretty much passed away. While there are still some pimps who dress up and drive expensive cars, many others are characterized by police as "shitbirds," people who are dirty, unkempt, and in need of a bath. Pimps will brutalize prostitutes, but their main source of control is drugs. They will attempt to get a new recruit on drugs, particularly heroin, which is quite addictive. Once this addiction is achieved and the pimp controls the heroin supply, the prostitute will do anything she's asked. "And she's finis," said one cop. "Her life is over."

The term pimp has uncertain origins but was first sighted in print in the 1700s. Ernest Weekly said in *Etymological Dictionary of English Language* (1921) that it might have come from *pimepeneau*, an Old French word defined as a "knave, rascall, varlet, and scoundrell."

Pimps are also known as *promoters*.

pimp your pipe

To lend or rent a *CRACK* pipe or stem.

pinch

Arrest.

See also *BAG, BUST, COLLAR, FALL,* and *KEEPER.*

pin job

Motor vehicle accident in which someone is trapped under a car.

pink look

The fresh-faced, innocent look of a new prisoner.

pipe bomb

Bomb made with a piece of pipe filled with black powder.

Bomb squad members say that three-quarters of all bombs produced are the pipe bomb type, which are capable of great destruction but relatively simple to make. A piece of pipe is filled with ordinary black gunpowder, such as found in shotgun shells, and then an "initiating" device, such as a fuse, wick, or wire, is attached and the bomb is ignited. As the black powder burns it generates gases that increase the pressure in the pipe until an explosion occurs, fragmenting and spewing the pipe metal, causing a destructive effect similar to a handgun.

See also *BOMBER.*

PL

Abbreviation for penal law.

plant

1. Evidence planted at a scene or on a person to get them convicted of a crime they didn't commit.

   It is well known among law enforcement personnel that some cops can be quite ruthless in the pursuit of *BAD GUYS* they cannot get by legal means. Typically, the plant will be a felonious amount of drugs. When the victim of the plant is arrested, everyone knows that the evidence is phony, except the judge and jury.

   Plants are also used to provide the leverage to make someone *FLIP.*

2. A device designed to start a fire some time after the device is installed.

   Plants may be electrical, chemical, or something as simple as a candle that burns down and ignites an *ACCELERANT.* Whatever, they are designed to give the *TORCH* time to be far away from the scene and to establish an alibi.

player

See *DRUG DEALER.*

plea bargain

An agreement made by a defendant to enter a plea of guilty to a lesser charge in exchange for having a more serious charge dropped.

Plea bargaining is commonly used to dispense some sort of justice while unclogging the courts. (The average *FELONY* case requires fifteen court appearances.) Some defendants plea-bargain because they will be sentenced far less severely, they don't have to endure the expense of a trial, and they at least know what they will be facing. Prosecutors plea-bargain in order to get a conviction and keep their work flow going. Judges accept plea bargains to keep their caseload down.

One police officer explained the process in Mark Baker's *Cops: Their Lives in Their Own Words:* "Armed robbery carries a penalty of five to twenty-five years. If you get convicted of armed robbery—if you don't get it plea-bargained down, which is often the case—and you go up for the crime, you're looking at two years and you're out. It's job security for me if you want to look at it that way. But it ain't right."

plead

To make a declaration in court of guilt or innocence.

pocket man

Someone who holds the cash proceeds for a robbery.

pocket prints

A wallet or wad of cash easily visible through a victim's clothing.

point man

In prison, an inmate who serves as a lookout for the coming of any rival inmates, guards, or others.

This term comes from the military and dates back to the turn of the century. Down through the years there have been numerous references to a point man, someone who leads the way into possibly hazardous territory.

point of impact

In traffic accident investigation, the exact point at which vehicles involved in an accident impact.

See also *BUMPER FRACTURES, DART-OUT ACCIDENT,* and *THRUST DIAGRAM.*

pop

1. Murder someone.
2. An arrest.

poppers

Ampules of amyl nitrite (commonly, *AMYL NITRATE*).

Amyl nitrite is an inhalant drug used to increase physiological functions such as heart rate and to increase sexual pleasure. Other street names include ames, amies, boppers, heart-on, and pearls.

poppy loves

Elderly Jewish men who are potential robbery victims.

This phrase, used most often by black criminals, arises out of the perception that Jewish children are always telling their fathers—their "poppies"—that they love them, or at least acting as if they do. When used by criminals, it is a pejorative, patronizing term.

Carsten Stroud refers to it in *Close Pursuit:* "This far down the line it was still home country. There were no 'poppy loves' . . . in the car."

portables

Officers on foot.

The sense of the term is that police on foot are much better able to move around than police in vehicles.

See also *BEAT COPS.*

posse

Jamaican gangs.

Posses are *GANGS* that started in the urban Kingston section of Jamaica. Jamaicans are avid moviegoers, and it is speculated that the nickname "posse" was adopted from the many American westerns that play in Jamaican theaters.

Posses have emigrated to various countries, including America, and primarily make their money by dealing drugs. They are as vicious as any gangs in the world. "There's nothing as bad," said the former head of BATF in New York City, "as a bad Jamaican."

Posses will readily shoot law enforcement personnel, and they have such little regard for human life that they have been known to hire people to run their *CRACK HOUSES,* then kill them rather than pay for the work. A variety of posses exist. Government efforts to stifle them have been made more difficult because posses are hard to penetrate with undercover operatives and the dialect poses a real problem. Even when the government gets members of posses on tape, it is difficult to tell what they're talking about.

post

1. Short for postmortem examination, or autopsy.

    An autopsy is totally invasive, surgically speaking. After the body is cleaned, a Y-shaped incision is made in the chest, the breast plate is removed, and the heart and lungs are examined and weighed; the abdomen is opened up, and the organs are removed for examination; and the skull is also sawed open and the brain is removed. Sections of the organs are taken for toxicological examination, and complete bloodwork is done, including screening for poisons. Following examination, the organs are returned to the body.

    It is important—and often required—that the main investigating detective (or "primary") be present at the autopsy, available to answer any questions the medical examiner *(ME or CORONER)* may have. The investigator's answers may be helpful in determining a definitive cause of death. When the examination is complete, the ME issues a written report called a *PROTOCOL.*
    See also *MAKE A CANOE* and *OPEN HIM/HER UP.*

2. Area patrolled by a police officer.
    See also *BEAT, FOOT POST,* and *SECTOR.*

postmortem

Latin phrase meaning "after death."

Investigators use this term to describe anything that occurred to a decedent after death.

pot

Marijuana.

Of all the terms for marijuana used on *THE STREET,* the most common is pot. (Perhaps the second most common term is grass.) The term probably comes from the Mexican *potiguaya,* a kind of marijuana leaf. Like other drugs, dealers have names for marijuana that describe particular characteristics that are meaningful to buyers. For example, "Acapulco Gold" and "African Black" indicate the regions where the pot was grown. Certain particularly potent types are associated with certain places; for example, "Culican" is a high-potency strain grown in Mexico, and "Citrol" is a high-potency type from Nepal. If the dealer is selling "Hawaiian" marijuana, the buyer will expect it to be very high potency. Other terms for marijuana include:

African bush
African woodbine
airplane
Alice B. Toklas (mari-
    juana brownie)
amp joint (marijuana
    laced with some
    sort of narcotic)
Angola
ashes
atom bomb (marijuana
    mixed with heroin)
atshitshi
Aunt Mary
B-40 (cigar laced with
    marijuana and
    dipped in malt
    liquor)
baby
bambalacha
bar
bash
basuco (coca paste
    sprinkled on mari-
    juana)
belyando sruce

bhang
black
black bart
black ganga (mari-
    juana resin)
black gold
black gungi
black gunion
black mo/black moat
black mote (marijuana
    mixed with honey)
blonde
blue de hue
blue sage
blue sky blond
bo-bo
bobo bush
bohd
bone
boo
broccoli
brown
bud
bullyon
burnie
bush

butter
butter flower
cam trip
Canadian black
canamo
crack back (marijuana
    and crack)
dope
el diabilito (marijuana,
    heroin, cocaine,
    and PCP)
esra
fallbrook redhair
fine stuff
fir
flower
flower tops
fraho
fry daddy (marijuana
    joint laced with
    crack)
fu
fuel (marijuana mixed
    with insecticides)
Fuma D'Angola
gage

ganja
garbage (inferior quality)
gash
geek (marijuana and crack)
Ghana
gold
gold star
golden leaf
gong
good giggles
grass
grass brownies
grata
green (inferior quality)
green goddess
greeter
Greta
griefo
griff
griffo
gungun
hanhich
has
herba
hocus
homegrown
hooch
Indian hay
Indian boy
indo
Jane
jay
jay smoke
Jim Jones (marijuana laced with cocaine and PCP)
jolly green
Juan Valdez
Juanita
kali
kaya

Kentucky blue
KGB (killer green bud)
kiff
killer
killer weed (marijuana and PCP)
kilter
kind
kumba
LL
lakbay diva
laughing grass
laughing weed
leaf
light stuff
little smoke
llesca
loaf
lobo
locoweed
love boat (marijuana dipped in formaldehyde)
love weed
lubage
M
Manhattan silver
Mary
Mary Jane
Mary and Johnny
Mary Warner
Mary Weaver
Maui wauie
Meg
Meggie
meserole
Mexican brown
Mexican red
MJ
MO
modems
mohasky

mohasty
monte
mooca
mooster
mootie
mootos
mor a grifa
mota
mother
MU
muggie
muggle
mutha
OJ
pakalolo
Pakistani black
Panama cut
Panama gold
Panama red (PR)
parsley
pat
pin
pod
potten bush
pretendica
Queen Anne's lace
railroad weed
rainy day woman
rasta weed
red cross
red dirt
reefer
righteous bush
root
rope
ross marie
salt and pepper
Santa Marta
sasfras
scissors
seeds
sen
sense

sensemilla	taima	viper's weed
sess	takkouri	wac (PCP on mari-
sezz	tea	juana)
shake	Tex-Mex	wacky seed
siddi	Texas pot	weed
skunk	Texas tea	weed tea
smoke	Thai sticks (bundles of	wheat
smoke Canada	marijuana soaked in	white-haired lady
snop	hashish oil; mari-	woolas (crack sprin-
splim	juana buds bound	kled on a marijuana
square mackerel	on short sections of	cigarette)
squirrel (PCP and mar-	bamboo)	X
ijuana, sprinkled	thirteen	yeh
with cocaine and	thumb	yellow submarine
smoked)	torch	yen pop
stack	torpedo (marijuana	yerba
stems	and crack)	yesca
stick	turbo (marijuana and	yesco
stink weed	crack)	Zacatecas purple
sugar weed	twist (marijuana ciga-	zambi
super grass	rette)	zig-zag man
sweet lucy	twistum (marijuana	zoom (marijuana laced
T	cigarette)	with PCP)

pound dealer

See *DOPE DEALER.*

pour patterns

Patterns in the path of a fire that may indicate the use of an *ACCEL-ERANT.*

Arson investigation is a sophisticated job that requires lots of experience. One of the things that investigators will look for after a fire are the pour patterns. For example, if they see that there was a fire on one side of a room, then no evidence of fire in the middle of the room, but fire on the other side, they will ask "How did the fire get from one side of the room to the other without burning the middle area?" The obvious answer is that an accelerant was poured on one side of the room, then on the other, then the two separate places were ignited.

power assurance rapist

See *GENTLEMAN RAPIST.*

precinct

A geographic division for which a specific group of police are responsible; also the station house itself.

The word precinct dates from the 1500s, when it was used to describe areas outlined either by map lines or by walls.

When describing a precinct, police usually announce its numbers by single digits—for example, the 42nd Precinct becomes the "four two," the 110th precinct the "one one oh." This is most likely done for clarity, especially when communicating on radio.

prima facie case

Latin for "on the face of it"; at first glance, used to describe a situation where a criminal case is sufficiently proven until contradicted by evidence to the contrary.

For example, investigators would have a prima facie case if called to a crime scene where they found a body on the floor and saw someone fleeing the scene, weapon in hand.

priors

Short for prior convictions.

When police arrest someone, the first thing they do is check for priors. They want to know just who they're dealing with. The check will also uncover any outstanding arrest warrants.

See also *HIT.*

probable cause

Sufficient reason to believe that a crime was committed; also called PC.

Probable cause is a key consideration when police are trying to get a warrant to search premises or a person. They must establish to the judge who signs the warrant that there is probable cause that the person or place was involved in a crime.

Some police get probable cause warrants after they search—that is, they will feloniously burglarize the premises, find what they want, leave it on the premises, obtain a search warrant, return, make a showy search, and then "find" the item again, this time all nice and legal.

profiling

A method for creating a psychological portrait of a *SERIAL MURDERER* or *SERIAL RAPIST,* based on crime scene details and the *MO.*

Profiling works best when used in investigations of bizarre killings. At such crime scenes, the criminals will leave more distinctive traces, some of which always indicate aspects of the criminal's character. For example, a lot of beating about the face generally indicates that the killer knew the victim; the more savage the attack, the closer the relationship.

Was the victim killed in a surprise attack? If so, it usually means a younger *PERPETRATOR,* because young killers usually feel threatened by victims and attempt to get them under control right away.

The FBI provides profiling services to police departments, and the more mysterious and motiveless the killing, the more useful it is for the FBI to get involved. All the local law enforcement agency has to do is fill out a very detailed questionnaire (actually multiple choice) about the killing and furnish photos and evidence as requested. The FBI doesn't claim prescience in discovering the killer, but profiling has certainly helped to keep local PDs on the right track in their investigations.

See also *VI-CAP* and *NCAVC.*

promoter

See *PIMP.*

prone out

The position suspects assume when they lie on the ground to be handcuffed.

protocol

A written report by the *ME* or *CORONER* that details the results of an autopsy.

Protocol is often used as a synonym for an autopsy, but it is simply the report that follows the autopsy.

The most important statement in the protocol is the opinion about the cause of death. But the report also tells how that conclusion was reached and provides details of the examination, including information on the external appearance of the body, evidence of injury, condition of the central nervous system, results of the internal exam, and anatomical and toxicological findings.

See also *POST.*

pruno

An alcoholic beverage made in prison from yeast, jam or jelly, water, and a fruit, usually prunes.

pugilistic attitude/pose

A distorted position a body takes when it is burned.

Many burned bodies are found frozen in this position, arms up and legs slightly bent, a sort of boxing stance. There is a myth that says that they are this way because they were symbolically, if not actually, warding off the fire. In fact, "the condition is caused by the natural contraction of the muscles as they are seared" (Vernon Geberth, *Practical Homicide Investigation,* 1990).

puller

See *MULE.*

pulling train

Gang rape; also known as *training.*

It is not an uncommon practice among gangs and is routinely done to women who join criminal motorcycle gangs.

pump

The heart.

In the most simplistic terms, the heart is a pump. It pumps blood to various parts of the body. Cops will use the term in a variety of contexts when talking about the demise of someone; for example, "He took two in the pump."

pumper

One who administers CPR.

This term relates to the fact that the heart is a pump. When police are working to revive someone, they are trying to get his or her heart pumping, hence the term.

punch job

A method of opening a safe by using a heavy hammer and chisel to remove, or punch in, the tumblers.

punk

1. In prison, a person who is a passive homosexual, usually a young male.

   This word is most frequently used in a sexual sense in prisons, where anyone who is gay is regarded as a punk.

2. A young, inexperienced criminal.

   Punks in this sense tend to have delusions of grandeur, criminally speaking, but do not amount to much in police eyes.

pusher

A person who sells addictive drugs illegally.

push shorts

To cheat in a drug deal; to sell an amount smaller than what is paid for.

put in a cross

See *JAM UP.*

puzzle

See *MYSTERY.*

PW

Policewoman.

Q

quarter

1. One quarter-ounce of drugs.

2. Twenty-five dollars' worth of drugs; also known as a "quarter bag."

queen

In prison, a "lady" or "girl," a man who dresses up and wears makeup like a woman and has a homosexual identity.

queer

Counterfeit money.

See also *FUNNY MONEY.*

R

rabbi

See *ANGEL*.

rack

To steal cans of spray paint.

Paint spray cans are on store racks or shelves, hence the term. Graffiti artists usually do the stealing, sometimes referring to the practice as "inventing" the paint.

Some localities lock up spray paint by city ordinance; others have it in the open, which makes racking much easier. Dedicated graffiti artists have been known to travel to unregulated states to steal the cans, then return to their home city to use them.

rack cells

Group of cells in a prison whose doors are simultaneously opened or closed by pulling a lever.

racketeer

Someone involved in a network of criminal activities, particularly those involving extortion or coercion.

Racketeers are gangsters in the grand sense. A racketeer is not someone who robs a gas station; rather, a racketeer makes payoffs, has *GOONS* to enforce his rules, and operates in a sophisticated way that results in large profits.

MOB members are the classic racketeers. The term was originally used to describe the Chicago racketeers of the 1920s. The word racket itself goes back a hundred years before that and was (and is) used to describe a *DODGE* or *RIP-OFF* of some sort.

RICO (the Racketeer Influenced Corrupt Organization Act) was specifically designed to put racketeers away, and it has done that magnificently. But from a criminal's point of view, RICO's overall effect on the mob is that of a healthy dose of bubonic plague.

radio talk

How police speak when in touch with dispatchers via patrol car radio.

See also *TEN CODE.*

rap

Criminal charge.

rape kit

A collection of items, including a comb and swabs, that allow physicians to take physical evidence from rape victims.

rape trauma syndrome

A psychological disorder suffered by rape victims.

Researchers Ann Burgess and Lynda Holstrom discovered that women suffer from rape trauma syndrome, in which the victim is psychologically haunted by the experience for years after the rape.

rapo

A convict who has been convicted of rape.

If his victim was an adult woman, a rapist is not looked at too harshly in prison, but it is quite a different story if the rapist has assaulted children (see *BABY RAPER*).

rat

An informant.

Rat is probably the most common term for an informant. It carries a sense of the despicability of the rat—ugly, vile, and vicious.

The term was not used to describe an informant until the early twentieth century. References dating back to the fifteenth century reveal that the term was used to describe a variety of people, including drunks, pirates, strike breakers, and the like. *Slang and Its Analogues* (J. S. Farmer and W. E. Henly, 1902) included the term in its present sense.

Cops use rat to describe informants, but without the other scurrilous senses of the word. It just means informant, perhaps because in the real life of the cop (as opposed to the TV/movie/book life), the informant is the cop's main tool for solving crime. Consequently, cops neither revere nor revile the informant.

ratpack

To gang up on someone.

rat's nose

Appearance of the nose after heavy cocaine sniffing has damaged it.

See also *BLOW*.

rave

A party designed to enhance a hallucinogenic experience through lights and music.

See also *BENDER* and *BREAK NIGHT*.

ray people

Mentally unbalanced people who falsely admit to committing murder.

After many highly publicized homicides, police get a variety of innocent people confessing to the crime. One Boston cop calls them the ray people, because they will often say that it was "rays from outer space" that made them do it. Sometimes their stories are believable and have to be checked out.

real estate

Living space in a prison cell.

See also *HOUSE*.

red-light district

Area frequented by prostitutes.

residence address

Police reference to where a person lives.

RICO Act

Racketeer Influenced Corrupt Organization Act.

This law was crafted in the 1970s to damage organized crime, and it has successfully done so. RICO is a success because it makes the proofs required to gain convictions much easier to get. Basically, all the government has to do is prove that an action is part of an overall pattern of crimes.

While simpler to prove, RICO carries hefty penalties—20 years and more for a single conviction.

See also *RACKETEER*.

ride

1. A car.

2. To shoot at someone from a moving vehicle; a *DRIVE-BY*.

ride the lightning

See *BURN*.

rigor

Short for rigor mortis, the stiffening of the body after death because of chemical changes in the muscle tissue.

Two to four hours after death, the body starts to stiffen. Most people think rigor begins in one specific area, but it actually starts throughout the body simultaneously, though it's easier to see in the jaw and neck area immediately. Within 12 hours the entire body is as hard as a rock. Within 18 to 36 hours the stiffness starts to disappear, and usually within 48 to 60 hours the stiffness is completely gone.

On TV and in the movies, rigor is often used by detectives and medical examiners to determine time of death. But experienced investigators will tell you that because of variables in temperature and other factors, rigor is not definitive. A photographer for the Tucson, Arizona, PD who had photographed hundreds of death scenes suggested, "The best way to try to determine time of death is to try to find the last person who saw the decedent alive, and when."

See *ALGOR MORTIS* and *STIFF*.

rip-off

A scam; to cheat someone.

The term had a patina of justification as used by the hippies in the 1960s. In *Good Housekeeping* (February 1966), Dr. Joyce Brothers explained that hippies regard ripping off the establishment as a political act. But after a while the activity was recognized for what it was—stealing—and the term picked up and retained a definitely negative meaning.

Where rip-off comes from is questionable. In the underworld there were "rip and tear mobs" who would accost people for their money simply by ripping their pockets off.

See also *CON.*

RMP

Abbreviation for radio motor patrolcar.

roach

The butt of a marijuana cigarette.

As a marijuana cigarette is smoked, the THC and other chemicals contained in cannabis resin gradually turn the paper brown. By the time the *JOINT* is reduced to the size of a butt, it is very brown and resembles an insect, hence roach.

A roach can be smoked quite far down. Smokers can place it in a holding device called a "roach clip" or in any sort of homemade roach holder that enables them to drag on the butt until it's almost nonexistent. It is common practice for a smoker to eat the minuscule remainder.

See also *JEFFERSON AIRPLANE* and *POT.*

roadblock

A barricade set up by law enforcement to stop or slow the traffic on a road for investigative purposes.

In the movies, roadblocks are usually designed to catch an escaped convict or dangerous *FELON.* But roadblocks are a standard police investigative tool. They will often set up a roadblock to stop and question potential witnesses about a possible crime in a specific area. For example, in Suffolk County, New York, in 1976, a young girl disappeared on her way home, and her body was subsequently found in a deserted, woodsy area a few miles from her home. She had last been seen alive walking down Caledonia Road at 5:00 P.M. on a Wednesday. For three days, police set up roadblocks along Caledonia for a two-hour period starting at around 4:30 P.M. and ending at 6:30 P.M. They stopped and questioned everyone to see if anyone had traveled along the road on Wednesday and, if so, had spotted the murdered girl, and when and where. The police hoped someone might have seen her getting into a vehicle and noticed something significant, such as the type, color, plate, etc. In this instance, it didn't work out; the case remains unsolved.

rockette
Female user of *CRACK*.

rogue cop
Police officer who doesn't follow standard rules and regulations.

The term is usually associated with police officers who are abusive to suspects and oblivious or relatively oblivious to departmental rules and regulations.

roll call
Calling off names of police officers to determine who is present for duty.

roll over
See *FLIP*.

runners
People who sell drugs for others.

running leads
Following *LEADS* in a criminal investigation.

running wild

Serving a prison sentence for which there is no minimum.

See also *BITCH*.

run up on

To steal from someone who least expects it.

This term is commonly used in the Los Angeles gang subculture.

sabot slugs

A one-ounce solid lead shotgun slug surrounded by a sabot, or plastic casing, which is the diameter of the barrel.

The sabot makes the shot very accurate even at long distances; there is no need for a specialized rifle barrel. While most commonly used for deer hunting, sabot slugs are favorites of anti-terrorist groups and SWAT teams.

This type of slug also has high penetration. *USA Today* reports that one ad for the bullets brags that "the slug had also penetrated a very high quality police vest."

safe house

A place where witnesses or other individuals are hidden to protect them against harm.

sam (a)

Federal narcotics agent.

satch

A piece of paper, letter, card, item of clothing, etc., saturated with drugs in solution.

Satch is one way drugs are smuggled to addicts who are being treated for their addiction in a hospital or other institution.

Saturday night special

A cheap handgun.

Such guns are often used in shootings, and many states allow easy access to them. The name probably comes from the fact that such guns are often used on Saturday nights, when drinking commonly leads to violence.

score
1. To make a profit from illegal activity.
2. To obtain drugs.
    See also *HIT.*

scratch
Money.
    See also *GREEN STUFF.*

screws
Term used by prisoners to describe guards.

scrip
Coupons issued in prison that serve as money.

search warrant
Legal authorization to search an area.
    See also *TITLE 3.*

secretor
Someone who secretes significant amounts of blood-group antigens in their body fluids thus allowing blood types to be determined from the secretions (semen, saliva, tears, etc.).

About seven-eighths of the population are secretors. The term made its first appearance in 1941 in the *American Journal of Obstetrics and Gynecology.*

sector
A segment of a precinct that is the responsibility of particular police officers.

Many police jurisdictions cut precincts into parts and call them sectors. Cars that patrol them are called sector cars.
    See *BEAT* and *POST.*

serial murderer
Someone who kills a number of people, usually one person at a time over an extended period.

Many people tend to confuse serial murderers with mass murderers, but the essential difference is that a mass murderer kills people all at once, whereas a serial murderer kills them over a long period of time, one by one.

In recent years serial murder has become as popular as Mickey Mouse in films, books, and mass media—there are even serial murderer collector cards. Many people have the mistaken impression that serial killing is a modern phenomenon, but serial murderers have been operating worldwide for hundreds of years.

The classic serial murderer of modern times is the infamous "Jack the Ripper," who in the late 1800s killed five prostitutes in the Whitechapel section of London. Today he would be characterized as an *ORGANIZED LUSTMURDERER* because of his devious nature and the mayhem he committed to the bodies postmortem.

There have been numerous infamous serial murderers in the twentieth century. In the 1920s, for example, there was Carl Panzram who killed 21 people. When he went to the electric chair, the only regret he expressed was that he wouldn't be free to kill more. And in the 1930s there was Albert Fish. While many people were shocked by the cannibalism of the recent serial killer Jeffrey Dahmer, Fish was even more notorious. He sent a letter to Delia Budd, the mother of a little girl he had kidnapped, in which he detailed how he had cooked and eaten the child over a nine-day period and had been in a state of constant sexual excitation.

Which serial murderer killed the most people is debatable. It is often said to be Henry Lee Lucas, a one-eyed drifter (a writer once commented that Lucas's glass eye was the warm one) who supposedly murdered over 300 people in the 1970s. This has been disputed, however, particularly by then Attorney General Jim Mattox who said that Lucas would confess to anything just to get favored treatment by officers anxious to *CLEAR* cases.

serial rapist

Someone who rapes a number of women.

This type of person, also known as a *pattern rapist,* is somewhat like a *SERIAL MURDERER,* except his crime is rape.
Sometimes, of course, rape leads to homicide, but murder is not the main motive of the serial rapist. Rape, no matter the type, is primarily a crime of power, control, and dominance; sex is used as a kind

of weapon. Horrific testimony to this is the regular rape of elderly women, who are not regarded by rapists as sex objects but as objects to be abused and controlled.

The term serial rapist was coined by the FBI's Behavioral Science Unit *(BSU)*, which also gave us the term serial murderers. The BSU keeps statistics on the movements of serial rapists just as they do with serial murderers.

Serpico (a)
See *BLUE WALL.*

set
1. A particular group of gang members.
2. A neighborhood or place where drugs are sold.

   Undercover police speak of being "on the set," and this refers, it would seem, both to the drug scene and to a set in the sense of acting, which is, of course, exactly what they are doing. (And they must be very good actors; their lives can literally depend on how convincing they are.)

shank
A knife or other sharp instrument used by prison inmates.

Prisoners are ingenious in making shanks. They have been constructed from everything from a metal bed slat to a toothbrush handle in which a razor is embedded. "At any given time," said one ex-convict, "there's enough shanks in a prison to open a cutlery factory."

Shanks are, of course, forbidden, and prison officials periodically seize them in random searches of cells.

shell corporations
Companies formed to launder money who do not engage in any other business.

See *MONEY LAUNDERING.*

shield
Badge of a law enforcement officer.

shine

Police term for a useless bureaucrat.

The term refers to the shine that bureaucrats develop on the seat of their pants from too much time spent sitting in chairs sliding around meaninglessly instead of actually getting up and accomplishing something.

shooflies

Members of PD internal affairs departments whose job it is to expose dishonesty in police officers.

Shooflies are generally despised by other police officers.

The term dates back to the 1880s when a "shoofly (man)" was a "criminal's spy, engaged in watching the police in order to warn the criminal of police activities. At some point the *IAD* man was given the sobriquet in what was obviously a disparaging way" (Eric Partridge, *Dictionary of the Underworld*).

See also *IAD*.

shooter

1. The person who fires the gun during the commission of a crime.

   Since around the thirteenth century the term has had a sporting definition, but in recent years it has had a criminal meaning. Today it is in quite common usage.

2. A drink of whiskey.

   Shooter is a common term among police for a strong drink. First use of the term was in 1971 in *Car & Driver* magazine: "He made his famous call for 'shooters.' Now in case you haven't heard, a 'shooter' is a variation of the word 'shot,' as in 'shot of likker' and . . . refers to a shot of Canadian Club mixed into a few fingers of 'Co-cola.'"

   See also *FLUTE*.

3. In some locales, a person who holds a dose of drugs and gives it to the person who bought it.

shooting board

Police and/or civilians who evaluate whether use of deadly force by police was justified.

Every police-related shooting incident in every jurisdiction of the country is investigated by and a determination is made by a shooting board to see if the officer acted within certain guidelines as they relate to the law in terms of justification, ethics, good judgment, and departmental policy.

In general, justice is done, but there is evidence of gross errors committed both ways—officers are excused when they shouldn't be and pilloried when they should be absolved.

shooting gallery

A place where drug addicts gather to inject drugs.

shoot up

See *MAINLINE*.

shoplift

To steal merchandise from a store.

See also *BOOST*.

shorteyes

A person who is sexually fixated on young girls.

The term probably comes from the idea that the person with the fixation only sees young girls, who are typically short or at least shorter than most adult women.

short-timer

Prisoner who has only a short time to serve on his/her sentence.

The term is generally used in other areas as well (such as a military person who has only a short time left to serve).

See also *GOOD TIME*.

shoulder surfing

Sneaking a look at someone's ATM (automatic teller machine) information in order to rob the account later.

Siberia

An undesirable precinct, station, or headquarters.

An officer can be disciplined in many ways by a law enforcement agency, and one way is to be shipped to what is generally known as Siberia, named after that Arctic-cold, forbidding place in Russia.

Siberia may be any number of things, but whoever sent the officer there knows that he/she will find it undesirable. J. Edgar Hoover was a great proponent of Siberia-style punishment. Anyone who drew his ire would find themselves in Tampa one day and watching caribou go by in Anchorage the next. Some commanders will take an officer off desk duty and send him/her to work a high-crime area—the shock alone is enough to kill the person. Or an officer may be transferred from one precinct in a city to another; the officer would still be working in the same city, but the commute would be doubled.

signal thirteen

In New York, the code meaning that an officer needs assistance.

Other locales have other signals to communicate this. Whatever the code, cops who hear it will respond instantly. Some people outside law enforcement who know the signal have used it to have officers quickly respond to a scene when, in fact, no police officer needs assistance.

sing

To inform on.

The term appears to have arisen from the concept of a bird in a cage: If the bird—a canary—sings it will get food. So, too, if a criminal who is in prison—a human cage—would sing out, or inform, he/she would also get a reward.

The term was common and popular in the early part of the twentieth century, but at this time is slightly archaic. Other words have taken its place, mainly *RAT* and *SNITCH*. *FINK* and *STOOL PIGEON* are also popular.

See also *INFORMANT*.

sit-down (a)

1. Mafioso getting together to discuss and resolve problems. Also known as a "table" or "meet."

2. Loan shark discussing the situation with someone who is deeply in debt to him.

sit on somebody

To conduct a surveillance on someone.

size the vic

Criminal terminology for sizing up a potential victim.

skeeger

See *BAG BRIDE.*

skeezer

See *BAG BRIDE.*

skeleton key

A key machined to open a variety of doors.

skells

Undesirable people.

skin popping

Injecting drugs under the skin.

skin search

The most thorough search of prison inmates, which involves removing the prisoner's clothing and possibly doing an internal examination.

skip

Flee illegally.

sky pilot

A prison chaplain.

slam dunk

Case in which the conviction of the criminal is simple, certain, and emphatic.

See also *GROUNDER.*

slam hammer

See *SLAPPER.*

slapper

Auto-theft device designed to pull out ignition cylinder so car can be started.

A slapper, also known as a *slam hammer,* was originally designed to pull dents out of cars. Hammering the device three or four times drives the existing cylinder out; the original cylinder is replaced with another one and the car can be started.

slim jim

A thin, flat piece of sheet metal with a hook designed to open locked car doors.

A slim jim is as basic to a car thief as a hammer is to a carpenter. The tool is slid down inside the door and its hook grabs the catch on the lock and pulls it free.

smack

Heroin.

Smack is one of the most common terms used for heroin. Smack has been around since at least 1960. Before this, in the early 1940s, it described a small packet of drugs. It is likely derived from schmeck, meaning a narcotic drug, a term that was borrowed from the Yiddish *smek,* meaning a sniff or smell.

smoke

To shoot someone with the intention of killing them.

Smoke is probably the most common word used by gangs to describe shooting someone, and police use it to some degree though not as much as *DO,* which is the most common word for killing or trying to kill someone.

Appropriately enough, smoke does not have a clear etymology, but is probably formed by the marriage of two concepts: the smoke a gun makes when fired, and the fact that smoke disappears much as the victim of a fatal shooting does.

There is reference to the term as far back as 1929. "Get inside and stay inside or I'll smoke both of youse off" (Jack Black, *You Can't Win*).

smurfing

In *MONEY LAUNDERING,* the process of making currency transactions to reduce a larger amount of money into negotiable instruments of less than $10,000 each.

In order to avoid reporting illegally made money to the IRS, drug cartels and other criminals employ launderers to "clean" the cash. Smurfing usually converts the large amounts into money orders under $10,000 each, the amount below which nothing is required to be reported. People who actually do the converting are called "smurfs."

The term comes from the energetic little blue television cartoon characters of the mid-1980s. Chuck Sapphos, a lawyer in the Department of Justice, was explaining the process of laundering money to his young daughter, and said that the people who did the work would typically have to run from bank to bank to do it. "Oh," his daughter said, "they're like smurfs." And the name stuck.

sniffer dog

Dog who is trained to detect drugs or explosives.

Dogs have very acute smell and so are excellent, when trained, at being able to detect drugs or explosives. Criminals who are aware of and wary of sniffer dogs will try to disguise or otherwise barricade the smell of the contraband so that it eludes the canines.

The term made its first written appearance in 1962 when the *New York Times Magazine* referred to "Sniffer, police dog."

See also *BOMB DOG.*

snitch

An *INFORMANT.*

The low man in the criminal aristocracy. Even Dante Alighieri didn't like snitches. In his epic poem *The Inferno,* he relegated them to the lowest point in Hell, where they were made to stand up to their waist in ice.

snitch jacket

A reputation, in prison, of being an informer.

snoop

An investigator, either private or otherwise.

Though this term is associated with detectives who are part of law enforcement, one more often hears police using it to describe private detectives. It was defined in 1949 in *American Folklore:* "The word I have frequently heard in New England, used both as a verb and as a noun. It implies sneaking, spying, prying around."

The word may have come from the Dutch word *snoepen,* which means servants and others whom, as *Oxford English*

Dictionary says, "appropriate and consume dainties in a clandestine manner."

snooperscope

A device that enables the user to see things at night much better than with the naked eye.

The snooperscope converts infrared radiation into a visible image; in other words, it shows radiated heat, which gives substance and form to people or objects being observed. The snooperscope is usually in the form of glasses or binoculars. Police regularly use them, although snooperscopes were not originally designed specifically for police use.

"The snooperscope can be used over a special helmet. It weighs from six to seven pounds and looks like something out of this world. . . . With one on his noggin, a jeep or truck driver could go barrelling down the road to the front without lights" (*Times-Dispatch,* Richmond, Virginia, April 16, 1946).

soles

See *HASH.*

solve (a)

See *CLEAR.*

speed

Amphetamines.

Speed is probably the most common term used by police to describe amphetamines. Characterized by law enforcement agencies as a stimulant, speed produces increased alertness, excitation, euphoria, higher blood pressure, insomnia, and loss of appetite.

The term dates from the 1930s when amphetamines were first used to treat narcolepsy, or sleeping sickness, the abnormal tendency to sleep during the day. Following this, many doctors prescribed them to treat a variety of disorders.

For awhile, amphetamines were sold without prescription, but abuse became rampant. They were particularly appealing to people who needed to stay awake for long hours, and many people became *SPEED FREAKS.* The prescribed dose of amphetamines is between 2.5 and 15 milligrams per day; those on a "speed binge" have been known to inject as much as 1,000 milligrams every 2 or 3 hours.

Speed has effects on the body that are physiologically similar to those produced by cocaine. Legally, amphetamines have limited therapeutic use, confined to narcolepsy, attention-deficit disorder, and in certain cases, as an adjunct for treating obesity.

Despite its risky effects, speed is a popular street drug, and laboratories produce tons of it for illicit uses. Other street names include

A
amies
amps
bam
beans
benne
benz
black and white
black beauties
black birds
black bombers
black mollies
blue boy
bombido
    (injectable
    amphetamine)
bombita
bottles
brain ticklers
brownies
browns
bumblebees
candy
cartwheels
chalk
chicken powder
chocolate
Christina
Christmas tree
co-pilot
coats to coats
crank
crink

cris
crisscross
Cristina
croak (metham-
    phetamine and
    crack)
cross tops
crossroads
crypto (metham-
    phetamine)
crystal
crystal meth
    (methamphet-
    amine)
dexies
diet pills
disco pellets
dominoes
double cross
eye-openers
fire (methamphet-
    amine and
    crack)
fives
footballs
forwards
French blue
glass
head drugs
hearts
horse heads
ice (methamphet-
    amine)

inbetweens
jam
jam cecil
jelly baby
jelly bean
jolly bean
jugs
LA (long-acting
    amphetamine)
leapers
lid oppers
lid proppers
lightning
little bomb
marathons
meth (metham-
    phetamine)
minibennie
nugget
oranges
peaches
pep pills
pink hearts
pixies
powder
purple hearts
quill
rhythm
rippers
road dope
robin's egg
Rosa
snap

snow
snow pellets
snow seals
    (amphetamine
    and cocaine)
Sparkle Plenty
sparklers
speedball
splash
splivins
sweets
thrusters
TR-6s
truck drivers
turkey
turnabout
uppers
uppies
wakes ups
white
white cross
whites
yellow bam
X

speed freak

Someone who severely abuses the use of amphetamines.

The phrase got its start in the 1930s when amphetamines were introduced, the name was given to people who reacted to the drug by exhibiting violent as well as bizarre behavior.

spike the job

A con game related to home improvements, in which jobs are started without authorization.

There are many *CONS* related to home improvements, but spiking the job is one of the boldest: A homeowner will contact a home improvement company to do a particular job, say to put new siding on the house, and the company will send a representative to the house to give a bid. The homeowners may or may not like the proposal, but will tell the contractor to wait while they consider it. The contractor, of course, is well aware that the delay may be because other bids are being considered—or that he's not getting the job.

Then one day, the homeowner comes home from work or whatever and gets a surprise: Old siding has been ripped from the house—the job has been started. Aghast, the frantic homeowner calls the contractor and explains the problem, and the contractor apologizes profusely—there was a misunderstanding—and asks what the homeowner wants him to do. Stop the job, or continue? Without much choice, the homeowner tells him that he might as well finish, which is exactly what the contractor counted on.

See also *THE WILLIAMSONS.*

spoon

One sixteenth-ounce of heroin.

square John

An honest person.

squeal

1. A complaint filed with the police.

    This is a common term in a host of police departments. Such departments also have a *squeal man,* someone who takes the complaint.

A squeal is more or less a prolonged, shrill cry, and its etymology would seemingly be based on the sound a typical *COMPLAINANT* would make. Though it might not be shrill in sound, it is at least shrill in emotional tone. Squeal was part of police lingo by 1949, when it showed up in Sidney Kingsley's *Detective Story,* a Broadway play that won an Academy Award when it was made into a powerful movie starring Kirk Douglas and Eleanor Parker. From the movie:

"This is Jim's squeal, ain't it?"

"Yeah, I'll take it. This is my partner's case. . . ."

One often hears the term used in conjunction with *CATCH—* catch a squeal. The appearance of homicide cops at the scene of a murder is mandatory, even though subsequent investigation is handled by precinct detectives who caught the squeal.

See also *BEEF.*

2. To inform on.

The term has been used since around 1872, but writers were still self-conscious about it in the early twentieth century. "Ever since his so-called 'squeal' at the Lexow investigation he has been a marked man" (*New York Times,* November 5, 1903).

The etymology of this meaning may relate to squeal being a complaint to the police. In a sense, if an informer tells the police something, it is a complaint also, because it reveals negative information about another person that can result in an investigation.

squeal man

See *SQUEAL.*

stakeout

A location chosen by police to observe and monitor the activities of the people associated with that particular place.

Also used as a verb. When police stake out an area, they are conducting a surveillance of the area or of people suspected of criminal activity.

stash

Place where valuables are hidden.

The origin of the term is not clear, but it has had criminal meaning since at least 1945, when Hellyner and Jackson wrote in *Vocabulary of Criminal Slang,* "it is used as a noun in the sense of something being cached."

statute of limitations

A statute assigning a certain time after which a person cannot be prosecuted for a particular crime, even if he or she is guilty.

Murder is the one crime that has no statute of limitations.

stay-in burglar

A *BURGLAR* who will hide on the premises of the establishment he or she intends to rob, emerging only after the establishment is closed.

Stay-in burglars still exist but are much less common than they used to be, particularly in the larger stores. The reason is dogs. Fifteen or 20 years ago someone got the idea to release dogs in a closed store just in case of a stay-in burglar, and word got to *THE STREET.* It's one thing to be robbing a store; it's quite another to be robbing a store while you're wondering whether or not a couple of Doberman Pinschers are going to come loping around the corner of the perfume aisle.

steerer

Confederate of a con man who helps convince others to play a game that is rigged against them.

The steerer usually plays the part of someone in the game and either wins or stands off to the side and gently urges the *PIGEON* to take part in the game. Steerers, who are also known as *cappers* and *ropers* are necessary to a variety of con games that require more than one perpetrator in order to be successful.

See also *BUNCO.*

stellate

See *CONTACT WOUND.*

step on

Cut or dilute drugs.

stick

Stab someone, particularly in prison.

stickup

Armed robbery.

The term describes what actually occurs: A *PERP* pulls a gun on someone and instructs them to stick their hands in the air so the perp can see them.

See also *HEIST.*

stiff

A dead person.

When death occurs, the body goes through a series of physiological changes, one of which is gradual stiffening, hence the term.

See also *RIGOR* and *ALGOR MORTIS*.

sting

1. Any police operation that involves setting up a situation in which criminals will be trapped and arrested.

   Some of the more creative stings in recent years involve alerting people who have been out on arrest warrants that they have won something but to collect it they must appear in person. When they do appear, they are arrested.

   For example, the Providence, Rhode Island, PD sent an invitation to various wanted people, telling them that they had been chosen to participate in the "promotion of Home Quality Entertainment Systems" and upon their appearance would receive either a color TV, VCR, disc player, or $100 in cash. The winners were alerted that they must first call to tell their confirmation number and the "prize you have won," and they would then be instructed "as to the date and time you may pick up your prize at the Providence Civic Center, located at One LaSalle Square, in downtown Providence, Rhode Island."

   "This is not a contest or lottery. You are guaranteed to receive one of the above fabulous prizes." What they won, of course, was a trip to court.

2. Various *CON* games.

stinker

A body in an advanced state of decomposition that smells terrible.

The process of decomposition begins at death. This consists of degeneration of the body and putrefaction, the breakdown of soft tissues by bacteria, fermentation, and the action of enzymes. Bacteria forms first in the gastrointestinal system, spreads to the vascular system, and soon engulfs the body.

Bacterial flora flourish in warm weather. Decomposition takes much longer in cold weather than in hot—people who had died of lead poisoning were found well preserved after being buried for 100 years in ice.

The smell of a stinker is one that police have difficulty describing, but one cop compares it to limburger cheese that has been left to rot. One way police endure the odor is to puff on cigars; another is to douse cotton with perfume and pack the cotton in one's nostrils; another is to place cigarette filters in the nostrils. Another, as seen on the TV show *NYPD Blue,* is to use baked coffee grounds.

See also *ALGOR MORTIS.*

Stockholm

To identify with one's captor when taken hostage.

The term, also known as the "Stockholm Syndrome," is used by hostage negotiators. It comes from an event that occurred in Stockholm, Sweden. A bank was robbed, and the robber—who was cut off by police—took three women hostage in the bank's vault. He subsequently demanded that his buddy be allowed into the bank. The police agreed, so now there were three women and two men in the vault.

They stayed there for six days, then gave up. During that time, the hostages and *HOSTAGE TAKERS* had gotten to know each other so well, and the hostages had come to identify with the *PERPS* so strongly that they refused to testify against them. In fact, two of the hostages ended up getting engaged to the offenders.

Police say Stockholming is good, because the offender also identifies with the hostage, and it's much easier to hurt someone you don't know than someone you do.

stone ding

In prison, someone who is mentally unbalanced.

stool pigeon (stoolie)

An *INFORMANT.*

"Stool pigeon" originally referred to a hunter's decoy: A fake pigeon would be mounted on a stool or other perch to lure birds who would then be shot by waiting hunters.

Then around the mid-1800s, professional gamblers began using it to describe their decoys, prostitutes, and others who would lead potential victims into bogus card games and the like, and police started using it to describe thieves who would inform on their own. The New York *Subterranean* of September 9, 1843, reported, "He appealed in turn to the police representatives then in attendance to a committee of 'shysters' from the tombs, and to a deputation of stool pigeons. . . ."

stopping power

The potential of a gun to render an armed offender motionless.

There are many myths associated with a handgun's stopping power. For example, it is said that forty-fives and guns having similar capacity impact so hard that they can spin victims around or knock them to the ground—stopping them.

No comprehensive studies have been done that show that any handgun is certain to have stopping power, but there is all kinds of evidence that even the heaviest weapons won't work in some instances. Experts say that the best tactic is to fire multiple shots to what is known as the assailant's "center mass" (the chest and area immediately above and below it) or to use a more powerful weapon such as a shotgun or rifle.

straight

1. A law-abiding citizen uninvolved in criminal activity.

    It is hard for some "straight" people to think that they would be looked down on by criminal types for this behavior, but criminals equate being straight with being stupid. The straight road is too long and hard—it's much easier to steal.

2. Someone who is not gay.

stranger rape

A type of rape in which the victim is assaulted by a stranger.

The rapist who is a stranger is much more likely to harm his victim physically than one who knows his victim. Typically, the stranger rapist has a weapon he uses to threaten his victim; he may also assault her with the weapon in addition to raping her.

straws

People who stand in for actual owners of businesses and shell corporations in order to hide ownership.

The term arises from strawman, or scarecrow.

street (the)

1. A general term used to describe the area where police officers work and learn and sometimes die.

   Police officers regard the street as one large classroom where they learn most of what they need to know about their trade. But as one officer put it, "The street can vary. If you're working in Beverly Hills it's one thing. If you're working the bad side of Detroit or the south side of Chicago or Bedford Stuyvesant in New York the street is different."

   The street is also a conceptual place, which describes the overall experience of being a police officer.

2. The world outside of prison.

street girl

On the West Coast and some other areas, a prostitute.

See also *CALL GIRL, GIRLFRIEND, GUMP, STREETWALKER,* and *WORKING GIRL.*

street person

Someone wise to the ways of the streets.

A term often used in prison—though it can be used on the street —to describe someone who knows "the score" on the street and is therefore fully capable of surviving on the street as well as in prison.

streetwalker

Prostitute who walks the streets to pick up *JOHNS.*

Life on the street quickly adds years to a streetwalker's appearance because she or he may perform 25 to 35 sex acts in an 18- or 20-hour day seven days a week, while taking drugs and not eating properly. Streetwalkers also have to be wary of dangerous clients, cops, and if they have a pimp, of getting him mad enough to beat them. Small wonder that cops say that women can look 10, 15, and even more years older than they are. *CALL GIRLS* have it much better.

The term has a long history. One written reference goes back to the 1600s but calls it "the world's oldest profession."

Streetwalker is, of course, euphemistic. Its origin is unclear. There are many references for the term in *Oxford English Dictionary*, but a line from an 1870 poem seems to be evocative in its simplicity of the entire experience: "On rainy nights thy breath blows chill in the street-walker's dripping hair" (Buchanan, *Poems*).

See also *GUMP* and *STREET GIRL*.

stressor (the)

The triggering event in a homicide.

Homicide investigators say that in most murders there is an event that makes it occur, be it the loss of a spouse or a job, or just that one person looked at another the wrong way. The stressor is the proverbial straw that broke the camel's back.

strip cell

A severe form of disciplinary segregation at a prison.

An inmate is stripped of clothing and then locked in an isolated room that is bare and forbidding. The lack of clothing and isolation tends to strip inmates of their sense of self, and the punishment is widely loathed.

See also *BLACK HOLE*.

strip search

Search of a person down to bare skin.

structuring

Arranging currency deposits in order to avoid reporting them to the IRS.

See also *CMIRs*.

stuffin' it

In female prisons, hiding contraband in the vagina.

In male prisons, contraband is hidden in the rectum. See also *KEISTER STASH.*

subject

The target of a criminal investigation.

Law enforcement lingo is sprinkled with euphemisms and dry language, and nowhere is this more true than the word subject. Cops may be following Jeffrey Dahmer, but they will always describe him as the subject.

The term may also be used to describe a car: "The subject vehicle is proceeding down Elm Street."

See also *OFFENDER.*

suit

1. A *BOSS* who has no value, an "empty suit."
2. A young college graduate with a career clearly marked for success.

suitcase

Drug capsules placed inside a balloon, or condom, then inserted in the anus or vagina in an attempt to conceal them from law enforcement personnel.

See also *KEISTER STASH.*

Superman syndrome

See *JOHN WAYNE SYNDROME.*

surveillance

The close observance of someone or something, done with or without the subject's knowledge.

suspect

Person who may have committed a crime.

SWAT

Abbreviation for a police department's Special Weapons and Tactics team.

T

tag

1. In prison, refers to a citation given by an official to a prisoner for behavior that breaks the rules. Tag may also refer to a reputation; that is, an official in a prison may be noted for disliking a specific behavior, such as homosexual behavior, and prisoners who practice what the officer dislikes will either avoid or confront him or her.
2. License plate.
3. Summons.

tail

To secretly follow a subject; to follow very closely is referred to as a "close tail."

The term arises from the idea that the person being followed has a tail attached—the person following. It first appeared in 1907 in *Everybody's Mag:* "The detective . . . assigned to tail him."

Tailing someone today as depicted in so many films can be a major military campaign, complete with a half-dozen cars, helicopters, and constant radio communication.

See also *BUMPER BEEPER.*

take flight

To illegally leave an area when charged with a crime and free on bail.

A person charged with a crime can often be freed by putting up *BAIL,* but is restricted from leaving a court-assigned area.

tap

To place a surreptitious device on a phone.

The term arises out of the sense of draining off something, like sap from a tree. E. Wallace makes reference to it in his 1923 book *Missing Million:* "How did you know where the tap was?"

In 1973 B. Murphy made a distinction between a bug and a tap in *The Business of Spying,* "As well as being 'bugged' a telephone can be 'tapped.'" A bug is a tiny device placed in a phone or a hidden spot, such as a lamp, to record conversation in a defined area. A tap is done only at the phone company and only under court order and can record only telephone conversation.

See also *BUG, PEN REGISTER,* and *WIRE.*

taste (a)

A small sample of a drug.

Tec-9

Short for the Intratec Tec-DC9 semiautomatic pistol.

This is a favorite weapon of drug dealers because it is a very effective killing tool. "That's all it's for," said an expert with the Bureau of Alcohol, Tobacco and Firearms.

It is relatively cheap even if bought retail, costing from $260 to $353 according to *USA Today* (December 29, 1993), but because of its appearance and firepower—it carries 32 shots—it can cost five times that on the street.

Experts say it is not a well-crafted gun, but it is deadly because it spews so many bullets in such a short period of time. Of all the weapons on *THE STREET,* police probably fear this one the most.

Ten Code

Radio code used by police departments.

Every PD has some form of radio code, such as a Ten Code, which they use to make sure information is transmitted speedily and clearly and cannot be understood by someone monitoring the broadcasts.

Such codes will differ from locality to locality. Here are some that the NYPD uses.

Ten 2   *Call the base.*
Ten 5   *Say again, please.*
Ten 6   *Be quiet, you're jamming the airwaves.*
Ten 7   *Away from car for lunch.*
Ten 11   *Audible alarm sounding in my sector.*
Ten 17   *On the way to your location.*
Ten 22   *Theft in progress.*
Ten 30   *Violent assault in progress.*
Ten 33   *Police emergency in progress.*
Ten 53   *Vehicular accident in my sector.*
Ten 59   *Fire alarm sounding in my sector.*
Ten 62   *Off the air temporarily.*
Ten 85   *Meet me at this location.*
Ten 98   *Car clear of assignments, ready for other duty.*

Ten 4 is perhaps the most famous of the Ten Code, having been popularized by actor Broderick Crawford in the 1950s TV series *Highway Patrol*. Crawford would frequently utter "Ten 4"—meaning I hear and will comply—and then zoom off in his patrol car.

testing for a tail

A movement a person makes to see if he or she is being followed.

To determine if someone is following you, do something that is unusual and see if the suspected tail does the same thing.

three-card monte

A classic card-game scam.

The game is played with three cards, as the name suggests. The dealer turns the cards face up, then asks players to keep their eyes on one particular card, say a queen of hearts. The dealer turns the cards face down and swiftly switches them back and forth, then stops and asks the *PIGEON* to pick out the queen of hearts. The pigeon thinks that he or she has an advantage, because prior to the game the dealer has turned one edge of the queen up, and the pigeon thinks that that's the card. But it isn't. The dealer will have turned that edge down and turned the edge of another up just before the game begins. The game has been around since the 1800s.

See also *BUNCO*.

throwaway

A suit or jacket worn by a mugger during the commission of a crime, then discarded as he makes a getaway, thereby altering the description the police may have of him.

throw-down gun

See *DROP GUN*.

throw in your papers

To retire from law enforcement work.

throw phone

Phone given by hostage negotiators to a *HOSTAGE TAKER* for communication.

To communicate with hostage takers, Chicago police throw them a phone in a canvas military bag, hence a throw phone. Otherwise, they might have to communicate via bullhorn, because one of the first things many hostage takers do is tear the phone out of the wall. Police used to throw a combat-style phone that had to be cranked to be used, but they decided this was too menacing. Now they throw in (as reported in *Pure Cop* by Connie Fletcher) a blue princess phone. And one officer said it has a "Smile—Have a Nice Day" sticker on it.

thrust diagram

Diagram used by accident investigators to help reconstruct an accident.

Sometimes it's difficult for investigators to determine exactly what occurred in a particular accident because there are no witnesses (driver and passengers may be dead) and not enough *PHYSICAL EVIDENCE*. In such cases, the thrust diagram is used. It consists of pictures of the scene and symbols of the car, which the cops move around on the pictures to help determine what happened.

tin
Police shield.

Shields are made of tin, hence the nickname.

Title 3
A court-ordered wiretap. Also known as a Title 3 Intercept.

toke
A single drag on a marijuana cigarette.

token sucker
In New York City, the name given to a thief who steals tokens from subway token machines by sucking them out.

Though token suckers have pretty much vanished from the scene, they once were—almost unbelievable but quite true—a force to be reckoned with in the city. They would jam paper into the slot where the metal tokens were deposited; then, while the patron went back to the token seller to complain that the stile would not open, or perhaps simply went through a different turnstile, the token sucker would press his lips over the slot and, vacuum-cleaner–like, suck the token out.

tool marks
1. The marks left by a tool on something during the commission of a crime.

   Sometimes when a burglar or other offender breaks into a place, he or she will use a tool that will leave a distinctive mark, such as a chipped pry bar. The slight defect can show on the material being pried.

   Investigators can usually lift these just like fingerprints. They make a rubber casting of the tool mark, then a plaster one.
2. *BITE MARKS.*

torch
A professional arsonist.

Cops say that there are two main motivations for arson: profit and revenge. Profit is often another name for desperation. For a businessperson who is losing money and facing a lot of debt and loss of the business, the only out may be to have the business burned down and collect the insurance.

Revenge may be motivated by anything, but it's usually the result of the rupture of a love relationship. One of the worst fires ever, the Happy Land Club fire in New York City, was started by an irate patron who had been thrown out of the club. He returned with a can of gasoline and doused the one stairwell—entrance and exit—and ignited it. There was no way out, and 89 people died.

A professional torch is not necessarily competent. The person hiring him may not know that the arsonist has no experience whatsoever—his only qualification might be that he's willing to torch a place—and that his actions will result in everyone being apprehended.

There is greater danger in using an inexperienced arsonist than using an experienced one. The experienced torch can set a fire so it is contained to some degree, whereas the inexperienced person can burn everything in sight, and more.

The torch must be quite good to fool arson investigators, because they can do a sort of fire autopsy that is as accurate in determining cause as the autopsy on a body. It would seem as if a fire would destroy all trace of everything, including hints that it was deliberately set, but this is not the case.

Reader's Digest referred to a torch in its March 1938 issue: "The torch is now serving a 20-year sentence."

See also *JEWISH LIGHTNING* and *MEXICAN LIGHTNING*.

tossed

When a place has been searched or burglarized.

Any place that has been searched or burglarized usually has one thing in common: It looks as if a tornado struck, with everything awry and tossed around.

People whose homes or businesses have been tossed feel a sense of violation, almost as if rape were involved. They weep, suffer sleeplessness, anxiety, and more.

toss the garbage

To search the garbage of a suspect for incriminating material, or leads to incriminating material.

The ordinary garbage of suspects can be extremely important to police. An excellent portrait of someone's life can be assembled by examining garbage, which can include old checks, bills, food receipts, food boxes, medication bottles, letters, bills, travel receipts, tickets, and so on.

Courts consider garbage part of one's home, and before it can be searched, *PROBABLE CAUSE* must be established and a *SEARCH WARRANT* must be issued. Of course, these restrictions are sometimes ignored.

Garbage often plays a vital role in the work of private investigators and others involved in divorce actions and the like.

tour

The shift or hours that police work.

Tours for cops vary from jurisdiction to jurisdiction, but in larger cities they usually are eight hours long.

tourist

An occasional visitor to a gay bar.

trace material

The physical minutiae that are exchanged or deposited when two objects impact.

The word derives from the sense that there are traces of material deposited when objects meet with some force. Typically, for example, when a car hits someone, there is physical evidence on the car, such as fibers and hair from the victim, and physical evidence from the car on the victim, such as paint and lens material.

Such evidence can be very important because of its nature: It is physical; missing sections fit into gaps. Many state and local departments do not have forensic labs large enough or sophisticated enough to analyze trace material, so they call on the FBI, who has state-of-the-art equipment and extremely well trained technicians.

Though valuable, trace material is not infallible. Matching hair and paint samples and fibers are not as conclusive as fingerprints, and there is always the possibility that the technician can make a mistake. Indeed, labs in Fresno, California, once sent back reports that said dog saliva was human semen.

And in some instances it is clear that any interpretation, when in a gray area, may be interpreted to favor the police. Still, trace material is important in helping to assemble a case.

See also *DNA, CIRCUMSTANTIAL EVIDENCE,* and *PHYSICAL EVIDENCE.*

traffic (a)

In some localities, a fatal motor accident.

trafficker

A major importer of illegal drugs, or someone involved in a big way in importing drugs.

Traffickers are thought of as being above the street-level dealer. A trafficker may be a multikilo importer (such as the Cali cartel), or an airline pilot, or a *MONEY LAUNDERER,* or someone who acts as a wholesale distributor (one who breaks down the products and distributes them to *DEALERS*).

traffic stop

When a police officer stops a suspicious person in a car.

As the authors of *Street Survival: Tactics for Armed Encounters* (Caibre Press, 1981) put it, "Few patrol events seem more 'routine' than vehicle pullovers, yet in an average year 12 percent of officers killed are shot while detaining motorists."

Pulling an ordinary person over for a traffic violation can sometimes trigger a violent reaction. Of course if the vehicle's occupants have been involved in a *FELONY* (see also *FELONY STOP*), the danger increases geometrically because it is highly likely that the occupants are armed.

Traffic stops are also characterized as nonfelony stops.

training

See *PULLING TRAIN.*

transvestite

A man who dresses up to look like a woman, or vice versa.

Also referred to as *cross-dressers,* transvestites are often confused with transsexuals, who actually physically modify their sex organs to become the opposite sex. Cross-dressing is not illegal, but police make themselves aware of it as part of the profile of a given individual because it may impact on an investigation in some way. Transvestites are often referred to by the initials *TV*.

trick

To work as a prostitute.

The origin of this term is unclear. The senses of fooling someone and performing some athletic feat perhaps feed into the meaning here. *Oxford English Dictionary* cites a rare meaning—to cheat someone of money—so perhaps this has something to do with it as well.

It is often said that a prostitute "turns tricks."

Claude Brown made reference to the term in *Manchild in the Promised Land* (1965): "Since her mother was laying so many cats, why shouldn't she be tricking."

See also *CALL GIRL, STREETWALKER,* and *WORKING GIRL.*

trip

A hallucinogenic journey triggered by taking LSD.

Also called trippin', perhaps because it is like taking a trip to another land—in one's head.

trolling for blues

Police officer dressing up as a potential victim and inviting attack.

This is a practice in PDs everywhere. It is frequently used where muggings or rapes are common. Both male and female officers troll; sometimes male officers dress as females. At least one candidate for the all-time record in trolling for blues is Bo Dietl, now a private investigator, who in his 20 years on the force posed as a victim more than 500 times.

tune 'em up

Police expression for an illegal physical assault.

An NYPD term that came to light during the Mollen Commission Investigation into police corruption in New York City. Corrupt cops testified that as part of their intimidation of drug dealers, one of their number would physically assault people, or "tune 'em up."

turkey

An undesirable *BAD GUY.*

One definition in *Oxford English Dictionary* is a "stupid, slow, inept, or otherwise worthless person." When police refer to people as turkeys, these characteristics seem to be understood. Not only is the person an undesirable in a criminal sense, he or she is also ineffectual: a small-timer.

The turkey, of course, is an admirable bird, but its main identity is as a slow, ungainly victim. In 1951 Harold Wentworth and Stuart Flexner referred to the term in *American Slang:* "So, if you got a collector (of internal revenue) through the civil service system who was a real turkey, you'd be stuck with that turkey practically until he died."

turn

See *FLIP.*

TV

Short for *TRANSVESTITE.*

tweaking

Drug-induced paranoia.

.22

A small-caliber handgun commonly used in organized-crime murders.

Though small in caliber, the gun is regarded by professional *HIT MEN* to be particularly effective. While its bullet will not drive through flesh like some others, its lack of power makes it particularly effective. Typically, the killer will fire into the victim's head. The bullet has enough force to penetrate the skull but not enough to drive through to the other side. It contacts and bounces off the inside of the skull, then bounces around, as it were, burrowing through brain tissue (which has the consistency of Velveeta cheese) and doing massive damage.

More than this, the gun is relatively quiet, and it is cheap and easy to obtain.

See also *GAT.*

U

UC

Undercover operative.

Unabom (or Unabomber)

A name given to an unknown person, believed to be male, who has been linked at this writing to 13 bombings across the United States that have injured 22 people and killed one.

Several of the bombs were mailed to specific targets: university professors, an airline company executive, an airline manufacturing company, and computer and service firms. The most powerful device was planted at an employees' entrance to a computer store in Sacramento, California, and resulted in the death of the store owner when he tried to move the device.

The FBI says the targets appear to have common links: individuals involved with airlines, computers, and aircraft production.

The Unabomber operates as if he were the evil protagonist in a novel. All the bombs he makes take a long time to build and are made with common substances such as string, tackheads, glue, gun powder, and batteries. Investigators say he has good skills in metalworking and electrical work. He is intelligent, as evinced most recently by well-typed, literate letters sent to the *New York Times*.

He is believed to be in his thirties, white, with reddish hair and a mustache. At this writing, he has been sending bombs for sixteen years.

uncle
1. In California gang lingo, the police. "Yo, there goes your uncle."
2. Federal law enforcement officer.

under the influence
Drunk or high on drugs.

This is the standard police terminology used to communicate that someone has consumed more than the legal limit in alcohol or has taken illicit drugs. It also means that the person is not capable of adequately controlling his or her actions, and is subject to arrest.

undesirables
Any group that appears to have a criminal intent or is potentially capable of criminal actions.

uniform
A uniformed police officer.

unmarked
An unmarked patrol car.

Patrol cars are painted in easily recognizable colors, but detectives usually use unmarked cars.

It is almost laughable, however, because most unmarked cars are as visible to *BAD GUYS* as a *BLACK AND WHITE* or blue and white. Such cars, perhaps so that they dare not have a hint of style, are super plain with chrome at a minimum and blah color that makes the car seem as if it came off the production line unfinished.

up against the stem
Addicted to smoking marijuana.

The stem refers to the stem of the marijuana plant. It also refers to a device used in smoking crack.

V

vampires

Police officers who work late *TOURS.*

Vampires only come out at night—they can't live in the sun—hence the term.

Many officers like late tours, either because it is convenient to their home life or because they are just night people.

The four-to-midnight tours usually see the most crime; the after-midnight tours are less active.

See also *GRAVEYARD SHIFTS* and *ZOMBIE.*

vertical patrol

Police officers who patrol apartment buildings.

vest

See *BULLETPROOF VEST.*

VI-CAP

Acronym for the Violent Criminal Apprehension Program.

An FBI program that provides a national clearing house for unsolved murders and arson. For murder, jurisdictions are asked by the NCVAC to fill out forms that ask highly detailed questions about unusual murders that have not been solved. Then, using NCVAC computers and sophisticated tracking techniques, the FBI tries to determine if the crimes are part of a pattern.

VI-CAP, which was the brainchild of Pierce Brooks, a former Los Angeles policeman, can be of great value because it is virtually the only way police can track *SERIAL MURDERERS* and *SERIAL RAPISTS* who travel from one state to the other. For example, if a redhaired woman in her twenties is killed in Baton Rouge,

Louisiana, that jurisdiction will likely not know that other states, say Mississippi and Alabama, have experienced murders of redhaired females in their twenties. But VI-CAP will know and can dispatch investigators to the scene for analysis and investigation, aiding local police.

Also available through VI-CAP is the Arson Information Management System (AIMS) for analysis of serial bombing and arsons under investigation by fire and law enforcement agencies.

See also *PROFILING.*

vics

Potential crime victims.

This term was popularized in inner-city New York, though it is occasionally used by anyone involved in criminal activity who scouts around looking for potential vics.

More and more, law enforcement is coming to believe that certain people are more susceptible to becoming victims than others.

vig

Exorbitant interest that *LOAN SHARKS* charge.

"Vig" or "vigorish" probably comes from the Yiddish *vyigrysh,* which meant gain or winnings. Earliest appearance is 1912. Said A. H. Lewis in *Apaches of New York,* "Stuss licks up . . . a round full fifth of all the east side earns, and to viggerish should be given the black glory thereof."

VIN

Abbreviation for vehicle identification number.

visual estimate

See *EYEBALL.*

voice prints

An audio fingerprint.

Voice or radio prints can be useful in all kinds of cases where proof is required that a certain person was speaking. Voices can be analyzed like fingerprints.

VTL

Abbreviation for vehicular traffic law.

W

wagon guys

In the Midwest, personnel from the coroner's or medical examiner's offices.

walk and turn

The walk that a person suspected of being drunk is required to make.

walk the cat back

The process of retracing exactly how a *MOLE* worked his or her way into an intelligence organization.

wallbangers

See *LUDES*.

wannabes

Low-level mafiosi who want to be *MADE MEN*.

war wagon

Midwest term for an armored personnel carrier.

A war wagon carries everything but the proverbial kitchen sink for mounting an armed assault, and its steel is so thick that it resists gunfire with ease.

wasted

1. Under the influence of drugs.
2. Murdered.

   Wasted was a very popular way to say murdered in the 1960s, but this meaning is seldom used today.

watering hole
See *COP BAR*.

weaver stance
A method of holding a handgun.

The normal combat stance for a police officer in firing a weapon is to have both arms extended the same distance with both hands on the weapon. The Weaver position, named after its California inventor, is a modification of this. One arm is slightly bent, and the other arm—the trigger hand—is straight. Proponents of this position say that it turns a handgun into a rifle, but there are arguments pro and con.

weight dealer
See *DOPE DEALER*.

wet floater
See *FLOATER*.

whack
Organized crime murder.

wheelman
The driver of a car involved in a crime.

It is unclear whether wheelman refers to the steering wheel of the car or the wheels of the vehicle, or perhaps both. It is clear that drivers of such cars are carefully selected for their skill and ability to take pressure.

The 1935 *Glossary of Prison Slang* by J. Hargan offers a simple definition of wheelman: "driver of a getaway car."

white-collar crime
Crimes committed by business people, which can range from stealing office supplies to big-time scams involving millions of dollars.

Once, the white collar criminal was someone who might bilk a bank out of money or a widow out of her savings, but today's thievery is commonly on a large scale. Though it is nonviolent, it can do damage to people that exceeds even violent crime. For example, if a group of investors is embezzled out of a lot of money, it can be hard to visualize the impact. When such criminals take a retired person's life savings or a major portion of his or her worth, that retiree has to go back to work or otherwise change their lifestyle to survive.

white money

In prison, currency.

Cigarettes are also very valuable in prison.

whodunit

See *MYSTERY.*

whore's bath

Washing the armpits only, or any other cursory bathing.

whore stroll

In the Midwest, areas where prostitutes ply their trade.

Detectives say that as a prostitute's fortunes decline (she gets older and less desirable, something that happens rapidly to even young women), her neighborhoods change. She might start in a very good area, but go to a less desirable one after a couple of years, and finally end her career—and perhaps her life—in a high-crime area where predators abound and existence is precarious to say the least.

Williamsons (the)

A roving band of con men who sell inferior home improvement work.

Just where the Williamsons came from originally is unclear (one theory says Scotland), but they are well known to police departments across the country. Anyone who perpetuates similar frauds are referred to as Williamsons. Their thievery has become part of the language.

The gang usually operates in the spring or other warm-weather months when homeowners are thinking about improvements. Typically, they will show up midmorning or midday when only the housewife is likely to be home. They will have on new work clothes and arrive in a truck that will also be in good shape. Their image is excellent.

They will tell the woman that her driveway looks in poor condition, and that if she likes they will seal-coat it to protect it against the wind and weather. And they will say, "Cheap. One can for $60."

The woman figures how can she go wrong, and gives them the go-ahead. Twenty minutes later they are finished and at the door asking for $600.

The woman is aghast, and says something like "You only said $60."

"Yes," comes the reply, "$60 for one can. We used ten cans."

The homemaker protests and the con men agree that because of the misunderstanding they will take $400. The woman agrees, reluctantly, then says she will give them a check. But they don't take checks, and they tell the woman they'll accompany her to the bank to get the cash. One goes with her, and she gets the cash, while the others stay at the house and possibly burglarize it.

And what did they put on the driveway? Either low-quality sealer or, in some cases, used crankcase oil that never really dries.

"These guys are slick," said one *BUNKO* cop. "Me and my partner were near the door while these guys gave their pitch to one woman, and I swear, when they were finished we wanted to know where do we sign."

See also *SPIKE THE JOB*.

window crash guys

Criminals who ram a vehicle into the glass front of a store, then quickly rob the store and flee.

wire

General term for an electronic device whose purpose is to secretly record conversation.

There are many different ways that wires can be used, but the most dangerous is to wear one. Today's criminals are alert to having their conversations recorded, and the person who wears a wire among them takes a big chance.

One of the scariest incidents was reported in the book *Prince of the City* where Detective Bob Leuci was wearing a wire and secretly recording conversation between himself and organized crime members. Then one of them noticed a bad smell.

Leuci excused himself to go to the bathroom. Inside, he stripped off his outer garment and carefully removed the wire, which had been leaking acid: The smell was his flesh.

Novelist John D. McDonald referred to the term in his 1957 book *Man of Affairs:* "The joint is wired, he says. The next step is cameras and infrared and tape recorders, I guess." Wired is itself a shortened version of "wired for sound."

See also *BUG* and *WIRE MAN.*

wire man

Anyone skilled in placing a recording device.

Most law enforcement entities have wire men, and these days they play a crucial role, particularly in the war against organized crime.

The public consciousness of what it takes to wiretap a telephone is erroneous. The popular conception is of a quick, furtive placement in a phone or on a wire close by; in fact, the wire man can tap a wire far from a subject's house.

In other instances, placing the wire must be quick and furtive and carries some risk of the wire men being discovered. One of the classic wires was placed one windswept, rainy night by New York State Police officers who succeeded in placing a bug in the Jaguar of the subject, a big-time mafioso named Anthony "Tony Ducks" Corrallo, who at the time was attending a wedding reception. Then Corrallo, feeling perfectly safe in his car, talked naturally and lugubriously about Mafia business to his driver, his conversation spiced with uncomplimentary references to some of his compatriots.

At one point in the operation, the bug, powered by the car's battery, started to fail because the battery was failing, and Corrallo brought the vehicle in for servicing—which would have meant discovery of the bug. But agents were able to get to the car and remove the bug, then replace it after the car was serviced. Corrallo, thanks to that bug, is currently in jail.

Police have also placed bugs in parked cars. In one Portland neighborhood, for example, police noticed that the bad guys they wanted so much never talked in an incriminating way inside a building. But each day they would stand on a certain street corner and speak openly. The creative solution was to park a car on that corner and leave it there: A tiny hole had been drilled in the trunk and the corner conversation was picked up by sensitive recording equipment inside.

See also *BUG* and *WIRE*.

wire transfers

Electronic transfer of money between financial institutions.

This is one way *MONEY LAUNDERERS* move their money without being discovered by law enforcement.

wise guy

A *MADE MAN* in the Mafia.

This has long been the preferred term among mafiosi and law enforcement authorities to describe someone who is in *THE MOB*. For years it was not that well known by the public, but Nicholas Pillegi's *Wiseguy* (1985) changed all that. It was the biography of Henry Hill, who had grown up in the mob in East New York, and who became a wise guy. Hill used the term frequently and almost exclusively to describe mafiosi. A motion picture, *GoodFellas*—another name for mafiosi—was based on Hill's book.

witness protection program

Government program that finds new identities for people who have testified for the government.

wood shampoo

Police using their batons to beat someone.

working four-to-fours

Male and female partners working a standard tour from 4:00 P.M. to midnight, then spending an extra four hours together off the job.

Police departments in general have a high rate of divorce (50 percent), and a male and female partner situation is said to be a contributing factor. Because their survival depends on each other, police partners are generally closer to one another than they are to their spouses. Consequently, the professional bond can change to romance rather quickly.

working girl

Prostitute.

Working girl is probably the most common term used by police as well as prostitutes and others in the trade.

See also *GIRLFRIEND*, *GUMP*, and *STREETWALKER*.

works

Equipment used to take drugs; drug paraphernalia.

Drug users use the following names to describe the various pieces of equipment.

Bong—pipe used to smoke marijuana

Carburetor—crack stem attachment.

Emergency gun—instrument other than a syringe used to inject drugs.

Feed bag—container for marijuana.

Fuete—hypodermic needle.

Gaffus—hypodermic needle.

Glass—hypodermic needle.

Glass gun—hypodermic needle.

Hype stick—hypodermic needle.

Paper bag—container for drugs.

Power puller—rubber piece attached to crack stem.

Roach clip—holder for partially smoked marijuana cigarette.

Rocket caps—dome-shaped caps on crack vials.

Satch cotton—fabric used to filter a solution of narcotics before injection.

Shaker/baker/water—material needed to freebase cocaine: shaker bottle, baking soda, water.

Sharps—hypodermic needles.

Spoon—tiny metal container, usually a spoon, used to prepare heroin for injection.

Stem—cylinder used to smoke crack.

Tools—equipment needed for injecting drugs.

XYZ

yard-out

Prisoner's time confined to disciplinary segregation, or the *BLACK HOLE*.

yellow sheet

In New York City, a record of convictions.

Today modern police departments are computerized, and New York City is no exception. But years ago all records were recorded manually, and convictions were recorded on yellow sheets of paper to differentiate them from other records—and to instantly indicate that someone had a record. The yellow sheets are long gone, but the term is still alive and well.

zombie

1. Police officer who works at night.
2. A heavy drug user.